Table of Contents

Furry Friends Quilt

Tooth Fairy Pillow — 12

Little Bow Sweet Quilt — 22

Duck Duck Tablerunner — 30

Knock, Knock, Who's There? Quilt — 42

Garden Fairy Sampler Quilt — 48

Strawberry Biscuit Fabric Index — 96

Furry Friends Quilt

48 ½" x 59 ½"

Fabric	Placement	Fabric Requirements
A to R	Background	2 ⅔ yards
S, T & U	Animal Faces and Ears	1 yard
V	Animal Hats	Three - Fat Quarters
W	Animal Bowties	Three - Fat Eighths
X	Animal Eyes	Three - Fat Eighths
Y	Animal Noses	Fat Eighth
Z	Animal Cheeks	⅓ yard
AA & BB	Flowers	⅓ yard
CC, DD & EE	Stems	⅓ yard
FF	Binding	⅝ yard
	Backing	3 ¼ yards
	⅝" White Ric Rac	4 yards
	Black Embroidery Floss	One Skein

Cutting Instructions

Background	A	8 - 4 ½" x 8 ⅛" rectangles
	B	4 - 4" x 11 ½" rectangles
	C	4 - 3" x 11 ½" rectangles
	D	28 - 2 ½" x 3" rectangles
	E	12 - 2 ½" squares
	F	12 - 2 ¼" x 2 ½" rectangles
	G	108 - 1 ¾" squares
	H	8 - 1 ½" x 13 ½" rectangles
	I	8 - 1 ½" x 12" rectangles
	J	4 - 1 ½" x 11 ½" rectangles
	K	8 - 1 ½" x 8" rectangles
	L	8 - 1 ½" x 3" rectangles
	M	16 - 1 ½" x 2 ½" rectangles
	N	64 - 1 ½" squares
	O	8 - 1" x 1 ½" rectangles
	P	16 - 1" squares
	Q	6 - 2" x WOF strips
	R	7 - 1 ½" x WOF strips
Animal Faces & Ears	S	12 - 7 ½" x 10 ½" rectangles
	T	8 - 3" squares
	U	16 - 1 ½" x 3" rectangles
Animal Hats	V	4 - 2 ½" x 9 ½" rectangles (from each Fabric V)
Animal Bowties	W	8 - 3" squares (from each Fabric W)
Animal Eyes	X	8 - Applique Pieces (from each Fabric X)
Animal Noses	Y	12 - Applique Pieces
Animal Cheeks	Z	24 - Applique Pieces
Flowers	AA	6 - 4" x 4 ½" rectangles
	BB	24 - 1 ½" squares
Stems	CC	6 - 2 ½" x 4 ½" rectangles
	DD	12 - 2 ½" squares
	EE	6 - 1" x 2 ½" rectangles
Binding	FF	7 - 2 ½" x WOF strips
⅝" White Ric Rac		12 - 10 ½" strips

Furry Friends Quilt

Animal Faces:

Using the Eye Template, Nose Template and Cheek Template, trace the facial features on the fabric. Templates are actual size and do not include a ¼" seam allowance.

Applique two matching eyes, one nose and two cheeks on each Fabric S rectangle.

Trim Partial Animal Face Unit to measure 6 ½" x 9 ½".

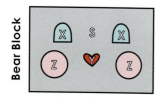

Make four.

Make four.

Make four.

Draw a diagonal line on the wrong side of fifty-six Fabric N squares.

With right sides facing, layer a marked Fabric N square on the bottom left corner of a Partial Animal Face Unit.

Stitch on the drawn line and trim ¼" away from the seam.

Repeat on the bottom right corner.

Animal Face Unit should measure 6 ½" x 9 ½".

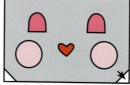

Make twelve.

Nose Template
Fabric Y
Cut 12

Eye Template
Fabric X
Cut 8 from each Fabric X
Cut 24 total

Cheek Template
Fabric Z
Cut 24

Bowties:

Draw a diagonal line on the wrong side of the Fabric G squares.

With right sides facing, layer a Fabric G square on one corner of a Fabric W square.

Stitch on the drawn line and trim ¼" away from the seam.

Repeat on the remaining corners.
Partial Bowtie Unit should measure 3" x 3".

Make eight.   Make eight.   Make eight.

Assemble Unit.
Bowtie Unit should measure 3" x 9 ½".

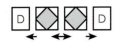

Make four.

Make four.

Make four.

Cat Blocks:

With right sides facing, layer a marked Fabric N square on one end of a Fabric U rectangle.

Stitch on the drawn line and trim ¼" away from the seam.

Repeat on the opposite end.
Cat Ear Unit should measure 1 ½" x 3".

Make eight.

Assemble Unit.
Cat Ears Unit should measure 1 ½" x 9 ½".

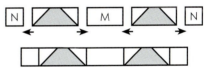

Make four.

Assemble Unit.
Partial Cat Unit should measure 9 ½" x 12".

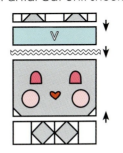 

Make four.

Furry Friends Quilt

Assemble Block.
Cat Block should measure 11 ½" x 12".

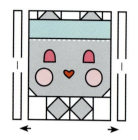 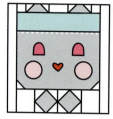

Make four.

• • • • • • • • • • • • • •

Bear Blocks:

Draw a diagonal line on the wrong side of the Fabric P squares.

With right sides facing, layer a Fabric P square on the top left corner of a Fabric U rectangle.

Stitch on the drawn line and trim ¼" away from the seam.

Repeat on the bottom left corner.
Bear Ear Unit should measure 1 ½" x 3".

Make eight.

Assemble Unit.
Partial Bear Unit should measure 9 ½" x 11".

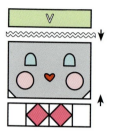 

Make four.

• • • • • • • • • • • • • •

Assemble Block.
Bear Block should measure 11" x 11 ½".

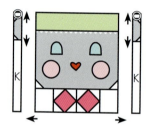 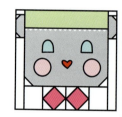

Make four.

• • • • • • • • • • • • • •

Rabbit Blocks:

With right sides facing, layer a marked Fabric N square on the top left corner of a Fabric T square.

Stitch on the drawn line and trim ¼" away from the seam.

Repeat on the top right corner.
Rabbit Ear Unit should measure 3" x 3".

Make eight.

Assemble Unit.
Rabbit Ears Unit should measure 3" x 9 ½".

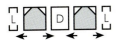

Make four.

• •

Assemble Unit.
Partial Rabbit Unit should measure 9 ½" x 13 ½".

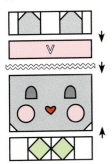 

Make four.

• •

Assemble Block.
Rabbit Block should measure 11 ½" x 13 ½".

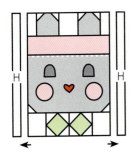 

Make four.

Embroidery:

To add the eyelashes and mouth, use the templates below.

Use three strands of embroidery floss and a backstitch.

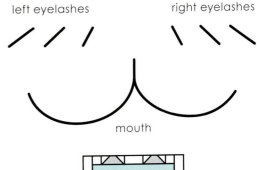

left eyelashes   right eyelashes

mouth

Make four.

Make four.

Make four.

Furry Friends Quilt

Flower Blocks:

Draw a diagonal line on the wrong side of the Fabric BB squares.

With right sides facing, layer a Fabric BB square on one end of a Fabric M rectangle.

Stitch on the drawn line and trim ¼" away from the seam.

Repeat on the opposite end.

Flower Petal Unit should measure 1 ½" x 2 ½".

Make twelve.

• •

With right sides facing, layer a Fabric G square on the bottom left corner of a Fabric AA rectangle.

Stitch on the drawn line and trim ¼" away from the seam.

Repeat on the bottom right corner.

Flower Head Unit should measure 4" x 4 ½".

Make six.

• •

Assemble Unit.

Partial Stem Unit should measure 2 ½" x 4 ½".

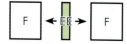

Make six.

Draw a diagonal line on the wrong side of the Fabric DD squares.

With right sides facing, layer a Fabric DD square on one end of a Partial Stem Unit.

Stitch on the drawn line and trim ¼" away from the seam.

Repeat on the opposite end.

Stem Unit should measure 2 ½" x 4 ½".

Make six.

• •

Draw a diagonal line on the wrong side of the Fabric E squares.

With right sides facing, layer a Fabric E square on one end of a Fabric CC rectangle.

Stitch on the drawn line and trim ¼" away from the seam.

Repeat on the opposite end.

Leaf Unit should measure 2 ½" x 4 ½".

Make six.

• •

Assemble Block.

Flower Block should measure 4 ½" x 9".

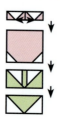

Make six.

Quilt Center:

Piece the Fabric R strips end to end.
Subcut into:
   4 - 1 ½" x 56 ½" strips

Assemble Quilt Center. Press toward the background.
Quilt Center should measure 45 ½" x 56 ½".

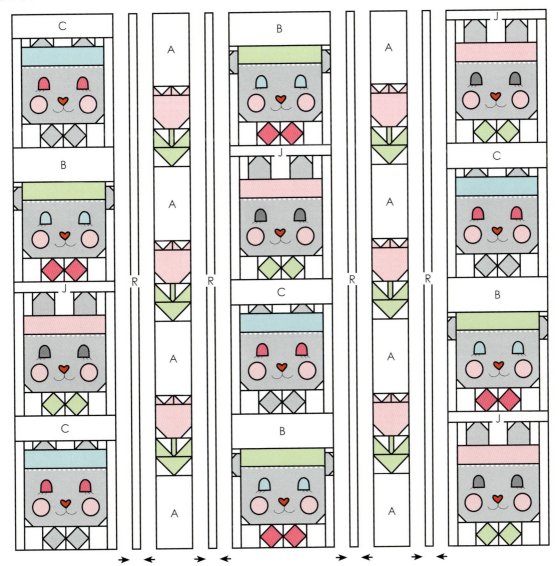

Furry Friends Quilt

Borders:

Piece the Fabric Q strips end to end.
Subcut into:

    2 - 2" x 56 ½" (Side Borders - Q1)

    2 - 2" x 48 ½" (Top and Bottom Borders - Q2)

Attach Side Borders.

Attach Top and Bottom Borders.

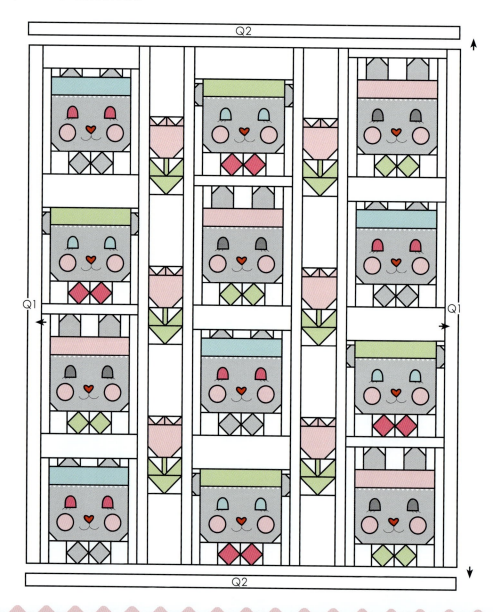

Finishing:
Piece the Fabric FF strips end to end for binding.
Quilt and bind as desired.

Tooth Fairy Pillow

14 1/2" x 14 1/2"

Fabric	Placement	Fabric Requirements
A to I	Background	1/3 yard
J to M	Skin	Fat Eighth
N, O & P	Hair and Shoes	Fat Eighth
Q, R & S	Fairy Wings	Fat Eighth
T	Fairy Cheeks	Scrap
U	Tooth Pocket	Scrap
V & W	Pink Dress	Fat Eighth
X & Y	Aqua Dress	Fat Eighth
Z to CC	Dress Sleeves, Borders and Binding	5/8 yard
DD	Backing	3/4 yard
	Muslin	5/8 yard
	Batting	Crib
	5/8" Pink Ric Rac	2 yards
	14" Pillow Form	One
	Brown Embroidery Floss	One Skein
	3/16" Black Buttons	Two

Cutting Instructions

Background	A	1 - 3 ½" x 5" rectangle
	B	1 - 3 ½" x 5" rectangle
	C	2 - 3 ½" squares
	D	2 - 2 ½" x 4 ⅞" rectangles
	E	2 - 2" x 7 ½" rectangles
	F	2 - 2" squares
	G	2 - 1 ½" x 3 ½" rectangles
	H	2 - 1 ½" squares
	I	1 - 1 ¼" x 2 ½" rectangle
Skin	J	1 - 3 ½" square
	K	1 - 2 ⅜" square
	L	2 - 2" squares
	M	2 - 1 ¾" squares
Hair and Shoes	N	2 - 2" squares
	O	1 - 1 ½" x 3 ½" rectangle
	P	2 - 1 ¼" x 1 ¾" rectangles
Fairy Wings	Q	1 - 3 ½" x 5" rectangle
	R	1 - 3 ½" x 5" rectangle
	S	1 - 2 ⅜" square

Cutting Instructions

Fairy Cheeks	T	2 - Applique Pieces
Tooth Pocket	U	1 - 2" square (Fussycut)
Pink Dress	V	1 - 3 ½" x 12 ½" rectangle
	W	1 - 2" x 3 ½" rectangle
Aqua Dress	X	1 - 2" x 3 ½" rectangle
	Y	2 - 2" squares
Dress Sleeves, Border and Binding	Z	2 - 3 ½" squares
	AA	3 - 2 ½" x WOF strips
	BB	2 - 1 ½" x 12 ½" rectangles
	CC	2 - 1 ½" x 14 ½" rectangles
Backing	DD	2 - 18" x 21 ½" rectangles
Muslin		1 - 18" square
		1 - 2" square
Batting		1 - 18" square
⅝" Pink Ric Rac		4 - 13 ½" strips

Tooth Fairy Pillow

Tooth Fairy Block:

Mark a dot 3 ½" over from the bottom left corner on the wrong side of the Fabric A rectangle.

Draw a line from the top left corner to the dot.

With right sides facing, layer the Fabric A rectangle with the Fabric Q rectangle.

Stitch on the drawn line and trim ¼" away from the seam.

Left Partial Wing Unit should measure 3 ½" x 6 ½".

Make one.

• •

Draw a diagonal line on the wrong side of the Fabric L squares and the Fabric Y squares.

With right sides facing, layer a Fabric L square on the bottom left corner of a Fabric Z square.

Stitch on the drawn line and trim ¼" away from the seam.

Repeat on the bottom right corner with a Fabric Y square.

Bottom Left Wing Unit should measure 3 ½" x 3 ½".

Make one.

Draw a diagonal line on the wrong side of the Bottom Left Wing Unit.

Pay close attention to unit placement.

Make one.

• •

Draw a diagonal line on the wrong side of the Fabric F squares.

With right sides facing, layer a Fabric F square on the top right corner of the Left Partial Wing Unit.

Stitch on the drawn line and trim ¼" away from the seam.

Repeat on the bottom end with the Bottom Left Wing Unit.

Left Wing Unit should measure 3 ½" x 6 ½".

Make one.

Mark a dot 3 ½" over from the bottom right corner on the wrong side of the Fabric B rectangle.

Draw a line from the top right corner to the dot.

With right sides facing, layer the Fabric B rectangle with the Fabric R rectangle.

Stitch on the drawn line and trim ¼" away from the seam.

Right Partial Wing Unit should measure 3 ½" x 6 ½".

Make one.

• •

With right sides facing, layer a Fabric Y square on the bottom left corner of a Fabric Z square.

Stitch on the drawn line and trim ¼" away from the seam.

Repeat on the bottom right corner with a Fabric L square.

Bottom Right Wing Unit should measure 3 ½" x 3 ½".

Make one.

Draw a diagonal line on the wrong side of the Bottom Right Wing Unit.

Pay close attention to unit placement.

Make one.

• •

With right sides facing, layer a Fabric F square on the top left corner of the Right Partial Wing Unit.

Stitch on the drawn line and trim ¼" away from the seam.

Repeat on the bottom end with the Bottom Right Wing Unit.

Right Wing Unit should measure 3 ½" x 6 ½".

Make one.

• •

Draw a diagonal line on the wrong side of the Fabric K square.

With right sides facing, layer the Fabric K square with the Fabric S square.

Stitch ¼" from each side of the drawn line.

Cut apart on the marked line.

Half Square Triangle Unit should measure 2" x 2".

Make two.

Tooth Fairy Pillow

Draw a diagonal line on the wrong side of the Half Square Triangle Units.

Make two.

• • • • • • • • • • • • • • • • • • • •

Draw a diagonal line on the wrong side of the Fabric N squares.

With right sides facing, layer a Fabric N square on the top left corner of the Fabric J square.

Stitch on the drawn line and trim ¼" away from the seam.

Repeat on the top right corner with a Fabric N square and the bottom corners with the Half Square Triangle Units.

Pay close attention to unit placement.

Face Unit should measure 3 ½" x 3 ½".

Make one.

• • • • • • • • • • • • • • • • • • • •

Draw a diagonal line on the wrong side of the Fabric H squares.

With right sides facing, layer a Fabric H square on one end of the Fabric O rectangle.

Stitch on the drawn line and trim ¼" away from the seam.

Repeat on the opposite end.

Partial Hair Unit should measure 1 ½" x 3 ½".

Make one.

Assemble Unit.

Hair Unit should measure 1 ½" x 9 ½".

Make one.

• • • • • • • • • • • • • • • • • • • •

Assemble Unit.

Top Partial Fairy Unit should measure 6 ½" x 9 ½".

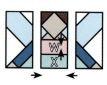

Make one.

• • • • • • • • • • • • • • • • • • • •

Assemble Unit.

Top Fairy Unit should measure 7 ½" x 12 ½".

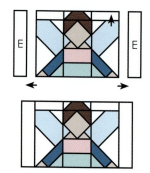

Make one.

Draw a diagonal line on the wrong side of the Fabric C squares.

With right sides facing, layer a Fabric C square on one end of the Fabric V rectangle.

Stitch on the drawn line and trim ¼" away from the seam.

Repeat on the opposite end.

Skirt Unit should measure 3 ½" x 12 ½".

Make one.

• •

Assemble Unit.

Bottom Fairy Unit should measure 2 ½" x 12 ½".

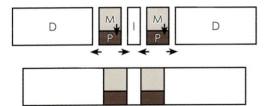

Make one.

• •

Assemble Block.

Tooth Fairy Block should measure 12 ½" x 12 ½".

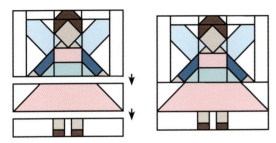

Make one.

Ric Rac and Borders:

Using a ⅛" seam, attach the ric rac slightly past the edges of the Tooth Fairy Block.

Trim excess ric rac.

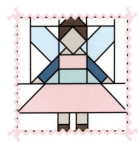

• •

Attach the side borders using the Fabric BB rectangles.

Attach the top and bottom borders using the Fabric CC rectangles.

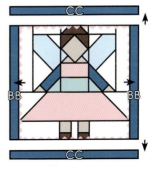

Tooth Fairy Pillow

Applique:

Using the Cheek Template, trace the cheeks on the fabric. Templates are actual size and do not include a ¼" seam allowance.

Applique two cheeks.

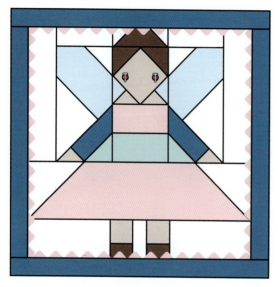

Embroidery:

To add the mouth and braids, use the templates below.

Use three strands of embroidery floss and a backstitch.

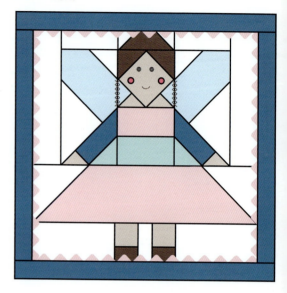

Buttons:

Attach buttons.

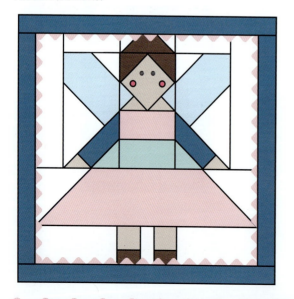

mouth   braid

Cheek Template
Fabric T - Cut 2

Tooth Pocket:

With right sides facing, layer the Fabric U square with the 2" Muslin square.

Stitch around the Fabric U square using a ¼" seam. Leave a ¾" opening at the bottom. Backstitch at the beginning and end.

Turn the Tooth Pocket right side out.

Press the opening edges under a ¼".

Make one.

Pin the Tooth Pocket to the Tooth Fairy Pillow Top.

Stitch the Tooth Pocket ⅛" from the edge on the left side, bottom and right side. Leave the top open.

Use matching thread. Backstitch at the beginning and end.

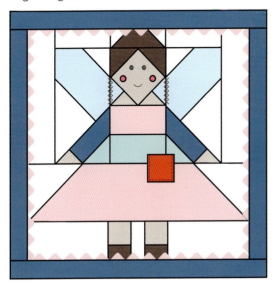

Quilted Pillow Top:

Layer the Tooth Fairy Pillow Top, the Batting and the 18" Muslin square.

Baste ⅛" around the inside of the Tooth Fairy Pillow Top.

Quilt Tooth Fairy Pillow Top as desired. Do not quilt over the Tooth Pocket.

Trim excess Batting and Muslin.

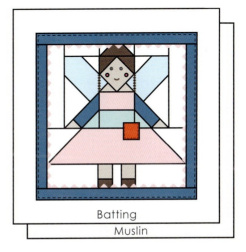

Pillow Back:

With wrong sides facing, fold a Fabric DD rectangle in half.

Partial Pillow Back Unit should measure 10 ¾" x 18".

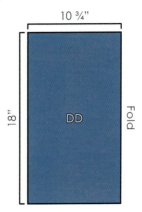

Make two.

Tooth Fairy Pillow

Pillow Assembly:

Layer two Partial Pillow Back Units and overlap them 3 ½" with folds in the center and raw edges on the outside.

Pin in place.

Pillow Back should measure 18" x 18".

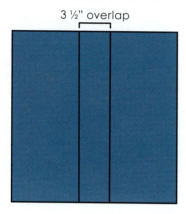

Finishing:

Piece the Fabric AA strips end to end for binding.

Bind as desired.

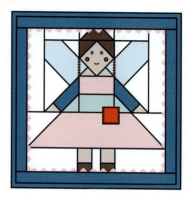

Mark the center of the Quilted Tooth Fairy Pillow Top and mark the center of the Pillow Back. Matching centers, layer the Quilted Tooth Fairy Pillow Top right side up on the Pillow Back.

Baste ⅛" around the edges to hold the Quilted Tooth Fairy Pillow Top and Pillow Back together.

Trim excess backing.

Little Bow Sweet Quilt

55 ½" x 66 ¾"

Fabric	Placement	Fabric Requirements
A to H	Background and Borders	3 ⅞ yards
I to L	Bows	Ten - Fat Quarters
M	Hearts	⅓ yard
N	Binding	⅝ yard
	Backing	4 ¼ yards

Cutting Instructions

Background and Borders
- A 40 - 5 ¼" x 8" rectangles
- B 15 - 3 ½" x 5 ½" rectangles
- C 20 - 3 ¼" x 7" rectangles
- D 15 - 2 ¾" x 3 ½" rectangles
- E 20 - 2" x 3 ¼" rectangles
- F 70 - 2" squares
- G 60 - 1 ¼" squares
- H 12 - 3" x WOF strips

Bows
- I 2 - 5 ¼" x 8" rectangles (from each Fabric I)
- J 2 - 5 ¼" x 8" rectangles (from each Fabric J)
- K 4 - 4 ¼" squares (from each Fabric K)
- L 2 - 2 ¾" x 3 ¼" rectangles (from each Fabric L)

Hearts
- M 30 - 2" x 3 ½" rectangles

Binding
- N 7 - 2 ½" x WOF strips

Little Bow Sweet Quilt

Bow Blocks:

Draw a diagonal line on the wrong side of the Fabric F squares.

With right sides facing, layer a Fabric F square on the top right corner of a Fabric K square.

Stitch on the drawn line and trim ¼" away from the seam.

Partial Top Bow Unit should measure 4 ¼" x 4 ¼".

Make four from each fat quarter.
Make forty total.

• •

Assemble Unit.

Top Bow Unit should measure 4 ¼" x 10 ¾".

 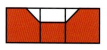

Make two from each fat quarter.
Make twenty total.

Draw a diagonal line on the right side of the Fabric I rectangles and the wrong side of twenty Fabric A rectangles.

With right sides facing, layer a marked Fabric A rectangle with a marked Fabric I rectangle matching drawn lines.

Stitch on the drawn line and trim ¼" above the seam.

Using the template, trim the Left Streamer Unit to measure 4 ¼" x 7".

Follow placement instructions on the template.

Make two from each fat quarter.
Make twenty total.

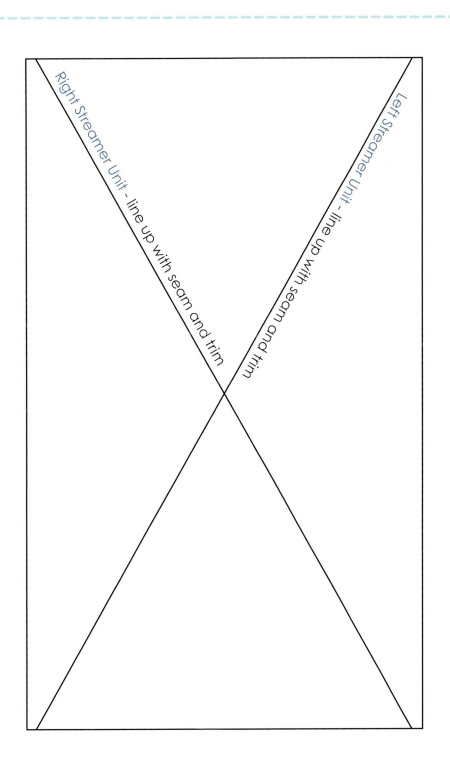

Little Bow Sweet Quilt

Draw a diagonal line on the right side of the remaining Fabric A rectangles and the wrong side of the Fabric J rectangles.

With right sides facing, layer a marked Fabric J rectangle with a marked Fabric A rectangle matching drawn lines.

Stitch on the drawn line and trim ¼" below the seam.

Using the template, trim the Right Streamer Unit to measure 4 ¼" x 7".

Follow placement instructions on the template.

Make two from each fat quarter.
Make twenty total.

Assemble Unit.
Bottom Bow Unit should measure 7" x 10 ¾".

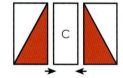 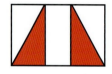

Make two from each fat quarter.
Make twenty total.

Assemble Block.
Bow Block should measure 10 ¾" x 10 ¾".

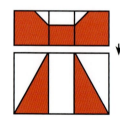 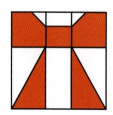

Make two from each fat quarter.
Make twenty total.

Heart Blocks:

Draw a diagonal line on the wrong side of the Fabric G squares.

With right sides facing, layer a Fabric G square on the top left corner of a Fabric M rectangle.

Stitch on the drawn line and trim ¼" away from the seam.

Repeat on the top right corner with a Fabric G square and the bottom end with a Fabric F square.

Partial Heart Unit should measure 2" x 3 ½".

Make fifteen.   Make fifteen.

Assemble Unit.
Heart Unit should measure 3 ½" x 3 ½".

Make fifteen.

. . . .

Assemble Block.
Heart Block should measure 3 ½" x 10 ¾".

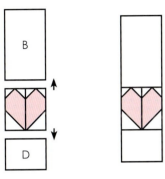

Make fifteen.

. . . .

Quilt Center:

Piece the Fabric H strips end to end.

Subcut into:

    4 - 3" x 50 ½" strips (Sashing - H1)
    2 - 3" x 61 ¾" strips (Side Borders - H2)
    2 - 3" x 55 ½" strips (Top and Bottom Borders - H3)

Little Bow Sweet Quilt

Assemble Quilt Center. Press toward the background.
Quilt Center should measure 50 ½" x 61 ¾".

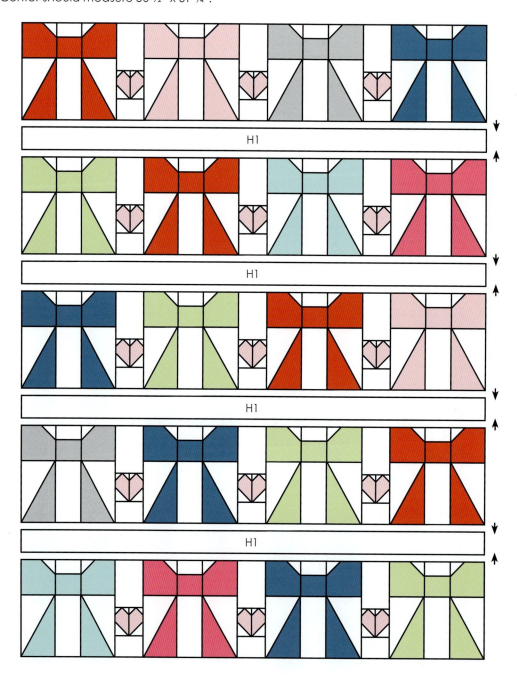

Borders:

Attach Side Borders.
Attach Top and Bottom Borders.

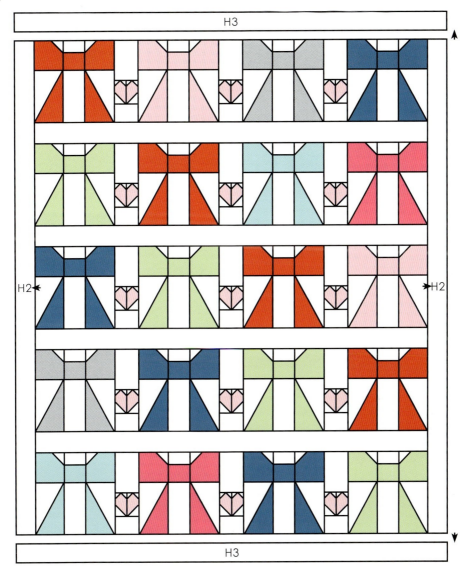

Finishing:

Piece the Fabric N strips end to end for binding.
Quilt and bind as desired.

Duck Duck Tablerunner

22 ¼" x 52 ¼"

Fabric	Placement	Fabric Requirements
A to R	Background and Sashing	1 ¼ yards
S to AA	Mama Duck, Lime Baby Ducks and Borders	⅓ yard
BB to EE	Aqua Baby Ducks	⅓ yard
FF, GG & HH	Diamonds and Borders	⅜ yard
II to LL	Mama Duck and Baby Ducks	Fat Eighth
MM & NN	Diamonds and Borders	12 - Fat Eighths
OO	Binding	½ yard
	Backing	1 ¾ yards
	7/16" Navy Button	One
	⅜" Navy Buttons	Five

Cutting Instructions

Background and Sashing	A	1 - 4 ½" square
	B	1 - 3 ½" x 4 ¼" rectangle
	C	5 - 3 ½" squares
	D	1 - 3" x 4 ½" rectangle
	E	5 - 3" x 3 ½" rectangles
	F	1 - 3" square
	G	5 - 2 ½" x 3 ½" rectangles
	H	5 - 2 ½" squares
	I	1 - 1 ¾" x 3" rectangle
	J	3 - 1 ¾" squares
	K	5 - 1 ½" x 2 ½" rectangles
	L	15 - 1 ½" squares
	M	10 - 3 ½" x 5 ½" rectangles
	N	4 - 2 ⅜" x 3 ½" rectangles
	O	24 - 2 ½" squares
	P	1 - 2 ¼" x 30 ½" rectangle
	Q	1 - 2 ¼" x 8" rectangle
	R	6 - 1 ¼" x WOF strips
Mama Duck, Lime Baby Ducks and Borders	S	1 - 4 ¼" square
	T	2 - 3 ½" squares
	U	4 - 3" squares
	V	1 - 2 ½" x 7 ¼" rectangle
	W	2 - 2 ½" squares
	X	2 - 2" x 6" rectangles
	Y	4 - 2" squares
	Z	2 - 1 ½" squares
	AA	4 - 1 ¼" squares

Cutting Instructions

Aqua Baby Ducks	BB	3 - 3 ½" squares
	CC	3 - 2" x 6" rectangles
	DD	6 - 2" squares
	EE	6 - 1 ¼" squares
Diamonds and Borders	FF	24 - 1 ½" squares
	GG	3 - 1 ½" x WOF strips
	HH	2 - 1 ½" x 17 ¼" rectangles
Mama Duck and Baby Ducks	II	1 - 2 ½" x 3 ¼" rectangle
	JJ	5 - 2" x 3" rectangles
	KK	2 - 1 ¾" squares
	LL	10 - 1 ½" squares
Diamonds and Borders	MM*	5 - 2" x 3" rectangles (from each Fabric MM)
	NN	2 - 1 ½" squares (from each Fabric NN)
Binding	OO	5 - 2 ½" x WOF strips

* You will not use all fabrics.

Duck Duck Tablerunner

Lime Baby Duck Blocks:

Draw a diagonal line on the wrong side of the Fabric L squares.

With right sides facing, layer a Fabric L square on the top left corner of a Fabric T square.

Stitch on the drawn line and trim ¼" away from the seam.

Repeat on the top right corner and bottom left corner.

Lime Baby Duck Head Unit should measure 3 ½" x 3 ½".

Make two.

• •

Draw a diagonal line on the wrong side of the Fabric LL squares.

With right sides facing, layer a Fabric LL square on the top left corner of a Fabric H square.

Stitch on the drawn line and trim ¼" away from the seam.

Repeat on the bottom left corner.

Lime Baby Duck Beak Unit should measure 2 ½" x 2 ½".

Make two.

Assemble Unit.

Top Lime Baby Duck Unit should measure 3 ½" x 8".

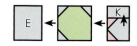 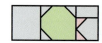

Make two.

• •

Draw a diagonal line on the wrong side of the Fabric AA squares.

With right sides facing, layer a Fabric AA square on the top left corner of a Fabric JJ rectangle.

Stitch on the drawn line and trim ¼" away from the seam.

Repeat on the bottom left corner.

Lime Baby Duck Wing Unit should measure 2" x 3".

Make two.

• •

Assemble Unit.

Partial Lime Baby Duck Body Unit should measure 3 ½" x 6".

Make two.

Draw a diagonal line on the wrong side of the Fabric C squares.

With right sides facing, layer a Fabric C square on the left end of a Partial Lime Baby Duck Body Unit.

Stitch on the drawn line and trim ¼" away from the seam.

Lime Baby Duck Body Unit should measure 3 ½" x 6".

Make two.

• •

Assemble Block.

Lime Baby Duck Block should measure 6 ½" x 8".

Make two.

• •

Aqua Baby Duck Blocks:

With right sides facing, layer a Fabric L square on the top left corner of a Fabric BB square.

Stitch on the drawn line and trim ¼" away from the seam.

Repeat on the top right corner and bottom left corner.

Aqua Baby Duck Head Unit should measure 3 ½" x 3 ½".

Make three.

With right sides facing, layer a Fabric LL square on the top left corner of a Fabric H square.

Stitch on the drawn line and trim ¼" away from the seam.

Repeat on the bottom left corner.

Aqua Baby Duck Beak Unit should measure 2 ½" x 2 ½".

Make three.

• •

Assemble Unit.

Pay close attention to unit placement.

Top Aqua Baby Duck Unit should measure 3 ½" x 8".

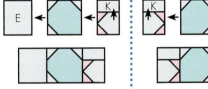

Make two
Left Top Aqua Baby
Duck Units.

Make one
Right Top Aqua
Baby Duck Unit.

Duck Duck Tablerunner

Draw a diagonal line on the wrong side of the Fabric EE squares.

With right sides facing, layer a Fabric EE square on the top left corner of a Fabric JJ rectangle.

Stitch on the drawn line and trim ¼" away from the seam.

Repeat on the bottom left corner.

Aqua Baby Duck Wing Unit should measure 2" x 3".

Make three.

- - - - - - - - - - - - - - - - -

Assemble Unit.

Partial Aqua Baby Duck Body Unit should measure 3 ½" x 6".

Make two Left Partial Aqua Baby Duck Body Units.

Make one Right Partial Aqua Baby Duck Body Unit.

With right sides facing, layer a Fabric C square on the left end of a Left Partial Aqua Baby Duck Body Unit.

Stitch on the drawn line and trim ¼" away from the seam.

Left Aqua Baby Duck Body Unit should measure 3 ½" x 6".

Make two.

- - - - - - - - - - - - - - - - -

With right sides facing, layer a Fabric C square on the right end of a Right Partial Aqua Baby Duck Body Unit.

Stitch on the drawn line and trim ¼" away from the seam.

Right Aqua Baby Duck Body Unit should measure 3 ½" x 6".

Make one.

- - - - - - - - - - - - - - - - -

Assemble Block.

Aqua Baby Duck Block should measure 6 ½" x 8".

Make two Left Aqua Baby Duck Blocks.

Make one Right Aqua Baby Duck Block.

Mama Duck Block:

Draw a diagonal line on the wrong side of the Fabric J squares.

With right sides facing, layer a Fabric J square on the top left corner of the Fabric S square.

Stitch on the drawn line and trim ¼" away from the seam.

Repeat on the top right corner and bottom left corner.

Mama Duck Head Unit should measure 4 ¼" x 4 ¼".

Make one.

• •

Draw a diagonal line on the wrong side of the Fabric KK squares.

With right sides facing, layer a Fabric KK square on the top left corner of the Fabric F square.

Stitch on the drawn line and trim ¼" away from the seam.

Repeat on the bottom left corner.

Mama Duck Beak Unit should measure 3" x 3".

Make one.

Assemble Unit.

Top Mama Duck Unit should measure 4 ¼" x 9 ¾".

Make one.

• •

Draw a diagonal line on the wrong side of the Fabric Z squares.

With right sides facing, layer a Fabric Z square on the top left corner of the Fabric II rectangle.

Stitch on the drawn line and trim ¼" away from the seam.

Repeat on the bottom left corner.

Mama Duck Wing Unit should measure 2 ½" x 3 ¼".

Make one.

• •

Assemble Unit.

Partial Mama Duck Body Unit should measure 4 ½" x 7 ¼".

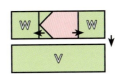 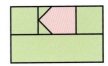

Make one.

Duck Duck Tablerunner

Draw a diagonal line on the wrong side of the Fabric A square.

With right sides facing, layer the Fabric A square on the left end of the Partial Mama Duck Body Unit.

Stitch on the drawn line and trim ¼" away from the seam.

Mama Duck Body Unit should measure 4 ½" x 7 ¼".

Make one.

• • • • • • • • • • • • • • • • • • • •

Assemble Block.
Mama Duck Block should measure 8 ¼" x 9 ¾".

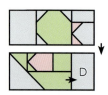

Make one.

• • • • • • • • • • • • • • • • • • • •

Buttons:

Attach buttons. Use the ⁷⁄₁₆" button for the Mama Duck Block and use the ⅜" buttons for the Baby Duck Blocks.

Make two. Make two.

Make one. Make one.

Diamond Blocks:

Assemble Unit.
Four Patch Unit should measure 2 ½" x 2 ½".

Make one from each Fabric NN.
Make twelve total.

• • • • • • • • • • • • • • • • • • • •

Cut the Fabric O squares on the diagonal once.

Make forty-eight.

• • • • • • • • • • • • • • • • • • • •

Assemble Block.
Press toward the background.
Trim Diamond Block to measure 3 ½" x 3 ½".

Make one from each Fabric NN.
Make twelve total.

Quilt Rows:

Assemble Row.
Duck Row should measure 8 ¼" x 47 ¼".

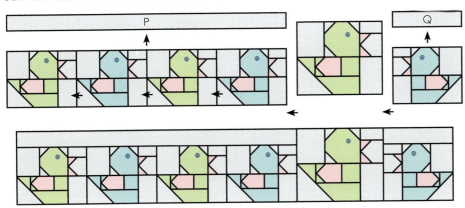

Make one.

Assemble Row. Press toward the background.
Pay close attention to block placement.
Diamond Row should measure 3 ½" x 47 ¼".

Make one.

Make one.

Quilt Center:

Piece the Fabric R strips end to end.
Subcut into:
   4 - 1 ¼" x 47 ¼" strips (Sashing)

Duck Duck Tablerunner

Assemble Quilt Center.
Quilt Center should measure 17 ¼" x 47 ¼".

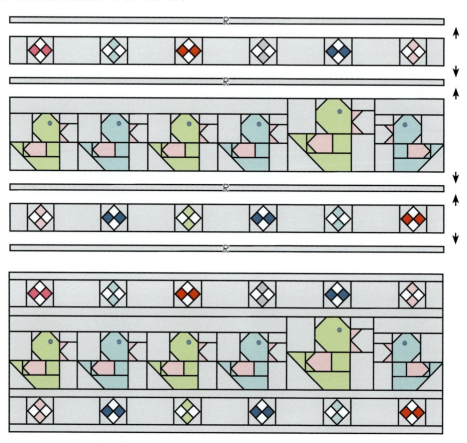

Borders:
Border fabric placement is intended to be scrappy.

Piece the Fabric GG strips end to end.
Subcut into:
   2 - 1 ½" x 47 ¼" strips (Top and Bottom Border)

Assemble Unit.
Trim Partial Side Border Unit to measure 2" x 17 ¼".

Make two.

Assemble Side Border.
Side Border should measure 3" x 17 ¼".

Make two.

Assemble Unit.
Trim Partial Top and Bottom Border Unit to measure 2" x 47 ¼".

Make two.

Assemble Top and Bottom Border.
Top and Bottom Border should measure 3" x 52 ¼".

Make two.

Duck Duck Tablerunner

Attach Side Borders.
Attach Top and Bottom Borders.

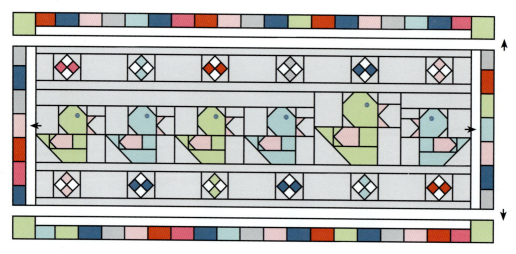

Finishing:

Piece the Fabric OO strips end to end for binding.
Quilt and bind as desired.

Pretty Playtime Quilts by Elea Lutz · 41

Knock, Knock, Who's There? Quilt

66 ½" x 84 ½"

Fabric	Placement	Fabric Requirements
A to F	Background and Sashing	2 ⅜ yards
G to M	Houses and Cornerstones	1 yard
N, O & P	Roof, Windows and Block Border	Three - ⅝ yards
P & Q	House Siding and Block Border	Six - Fat Quarters
P & R	Doors and Block Border	Two - Fat Quarters
P & S	Chimneys and Block Border	Three - Fat Quarters
T & U	Borders	3 yards
V	Binding	⅞ yard
	Backing	5 ¼ yards
	⅝" Pink Buttons	Twelve

Cutting Instructions

Background and Sashing
- A 12 - 5 ½" squares
- B 12 - 2 ½" x 4 ½" rectangles
- C 24 - 1 ½" x 11 ½" rectangles
- D 12 - 1 ½" x 5 ½" rectangles
- E 24 - 1" x 12 ½" rectangles
- F 31 - 2 ½" x 16 ½" rectangles

Houses and Cornerstones
- G 12 - 2 ½" x 5" rectangles
- H 20 - 2 ½" squares
- I 24 - 1 ¾" x 2 ½" rectangles
- J 12 - 1 ½" x 8 ½" rectangles
- K 12 - 1 ½" x 5" rectangles
- L 12 - 1 ½" x 4 ¾" rectangles
- M 12 - 1 ¼" x 4" rectangles

Roofs and Windows
- N 4 - 5 ½" x 10 ½" rectangles (from each Fabric N)
- O 4 - 2 ½" squares (from each Fabric O)

Block Border
- P 24 - 2 ½" squares (from each Fabric P)

House Siding
- Q 12 - 1 ½" x 2 ½" rectangles (from each Fabric Q)

Doors
- R 6 - 3" x 4 ¾" rectangles (from each Fabric R)

Chimneys
- S 4 - 3 ½" x 4 ½" rectangles (from each Fabric S)

Borders
- T 2 - 5 ½" x 74 ½" **length of fabric** strips
- U 4 - 5 ½" width of fabric strips

Binding
- V 9 - 2 ½" x width of fabric strips

Knock, Knock, Who's There? Quilt

Knock, Knock House Blocks:
Fabric placement is intended to be scrappy.

• •

Assemble Unit.
Chimney Unit should measure 5 ½" x 5 ½".

Make four from each Fabric S.
Make twelve total.

• •

Draw a diagonal line on the wrong side of the Chimney Units.
Pay close attention to unit placement.

Make twelve.

• •

Draw a diagonal line on the wrong side of the Fabric A squares.
With right sides facing, layer a Chimney Unit on the left end of a Fabric N rectangle.
Stitch on the drawn line and trim ¼" away from the seam.

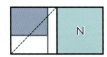 

Repeat on the opposite end with a Fabric A square.
Roof Unit should measure 5 ½" x 10 ½".

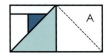 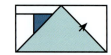

Make four from each Fabric N.
Make twelve total.

Assemble Unit.
Window Unit should measure 5" x 5 ½".

Make four from each Fabric O.
Make twelve total.

• •

Assemble Unit.
Door Unit should measure 4" x 5 ½".

Make six from each Fabric R.
Make twelve total.

• •

Assemble Unit.
Partial Bottom House Unit should measure 6 ½" x 8 ½".

Make twelve.

• •

Assemble Unit.
Bottom House Unit should measure 6 ½" x 10 ½".

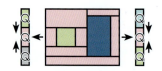 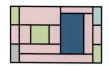

Make twelve.

Assemble Unit.
House Unit should measure 10 ½" x 11 ½".

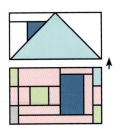

Make twelve.

- -

Assemble Unit.
Bordered House Unit should measure
12 ½" x 12 ½".

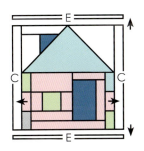

Make twelve.

- -

Assemble Unit.
Side Block Unit should measure
2 ½" x 12 ½".

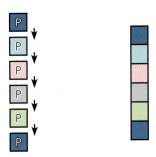

Make twenty-four.

Assemble Unit.
Top and Bottom Block Unit should measure
2 ½" x 16 ½".

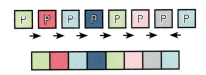

Make twenty-four.

- -

Assemble Block.
Knock, Knock House Block should measure
16 ½" x 16 ½".

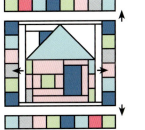

Make twelve.

- -

Button:
Attach button.

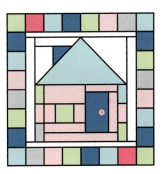

Make twelve.

Pretty Playtime Quilts by Elea Lutz · 45

Knock, Knock, Who's There? Quilt

Quilt Center:

Assemble Quilt Center. Press toward the sashing.
Quilt Center should measure 56 ½" x 74 ½".

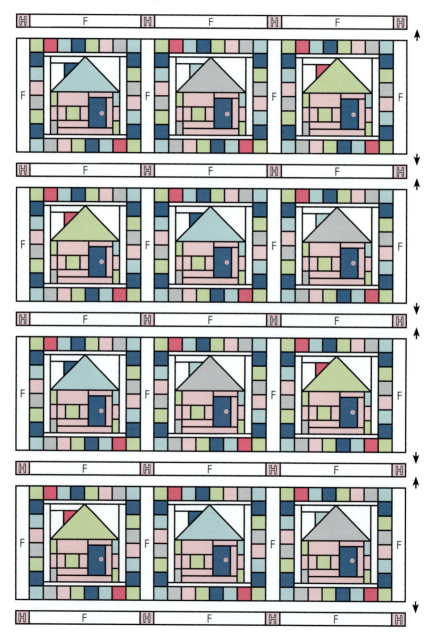

46 · Pretty Playtime Quilts by Elea Lutz

Borders:

Piece the Fabric U strips end to end.
Subcut into:
    2 - 5 ½" x 66 ½" strips (Top and Bottom Borders)

Attach the side borders using the Fabric T strips.
Attach Top and Bottom Borders.

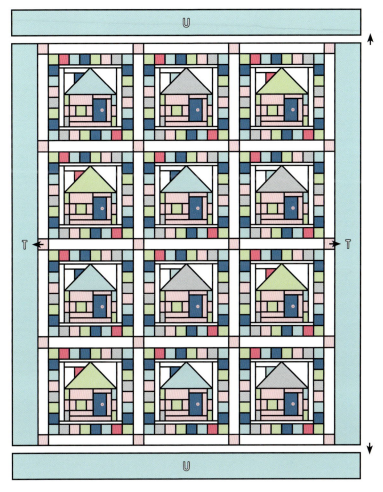

Finishing:

Piece the Fabric V strips end to end for binding.
Quilt and bind as desired.

Garden Fairy Sampler Quilt

74 ½" x 94 ½"

Fabric Requirements

C120-LATTE 10" x 10" Blocks	C120-LIGHTGRAY 10" x 10" Blocks	C120-RILEYBROWN 10" x 10" Blocks	C120-BLEACHEDDENIM 10" x 10" Blocks	C5105-GRAY 10" x 20" Blocks
C5102-GREEN 12" x 20" Blocks & Borders	C5102-PINK 12" x 20" Blocks & Borders	C5100-GRAY ¼ yard Blocks	C5104-BLUE ⅓ yard Blocks & Borders	C5100-HOTPINK ⅓ yard Blocks
C5103-RED ⅓ yard Blocks	C120-PETALPINK ⅓ yard Blocks & Duck Row	C5106-AQUA ½ yard Blocks & Borders	C5104-HOTPINK ⅝ yard Blocks & Flower Row	C5100-BLUE ¾ yard Blocks, Flower Row & Borders
C5103-GREEN ¾ yard Blocks, Duck Row & Borders	C5105-AQUA ¾ yard Blocks, Duck Row & Borders	C5104-PINK ¾ yard Blocks, Flower Row & Borders	C5103-PINK ¾ yard Blocks & Borders	C5106-RED ⅞ yard Blocks & Flower Row
C5105-GREEN 1 yard Blocks, Flower Row & Borders	C5102-BLUE 1 yard Blocks, Flower Row & Borders	C5106-BLUE 1 ¾ yards Blocks & Borders	C120-RILEYWHITE 10 yards Background	C5103-PINK 5 ⅞ yards Backing
10 ½" piece of ⅝" White Ric Rac	One ⅝" Pink Button	Five ⅜" Navy Buttons	One 7⁄16" Navy Button	Two 3⁄16" Black Buttons
One Skein Black Embroidery Floss	One Skein Brown Embroidery Floss			

Pretty Playtime Quilts by Elea Lutz · 49

Garden Fairy Sampler Quilt

Block 1
Dragonfly Block

Cutting Instructions

Background	A	2 - 4 ¼" squares
	B	2 - 3 ⅜" squares
	C	4 - 2 ⅝" squares
	D	1 - 2 ½" x 3" rectangle
	E	4 - 2 ⅛" squares
	F	1 - 1 ¾" x 4 ¼" rectangle
	G	3 - 1 ¾" x 3" rectangles
	H	2 - 1 ½" x 12 ½" rectangles
	I	2 - 1 ½" x 10 ½" rectangles
	J	1 - 1 ¼" x 1 ¾" rectangle
	K	1 - 1" x 2 ½" rectangle
	L	1 - 1" x 1 ¼" rectangle
Dragonfly Wings	M	1 - 3 ⅜" square (from each Fabric M)
(Two Fabrics)	N	2 - 2 ⅛" squares (from each Fabric N)
Dragonfly Bodies	O	1 - 3" square (from each Fabric O)
(Two Fabrics)	P	1 - 1" square (from each Fabric P)

Piecing Instructions:

Draw a diagonal line on the wrong side of the Fabric E squares.

With right sides facing, layer a Fabric E square with a Fabric N square.

Stitch ¼" from each side of the drawn line.

Cut apart on the marked line.

Small Half Square Triangle Unit should measure 1 ¾" x 1 ¾".

Draw a diagonal line on the wrong side of the Fabric B squares.

With right sides facing, layer a Fabric B square with a Fabric M square.

Stitch ¼" from each side of the drawn line.

Cut apart on the marked line.

Large Half Square Triangle Unit should measure 3" x 3".

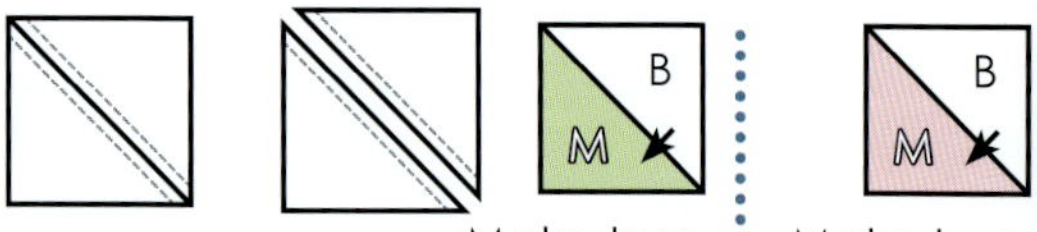

Make four.   Make four.   Make two.   Make two.

Assemble Unit.
Left Wing should measure 3" x 4 ¼".

Make one.   Make one.

Assemble Unit.
Right Wing should measure 3" x 4 ¼".

Make one.   Make one.

Draw a diagonal line on the wrong side of the Fabric C squares.

With right sides facing, layer a Fabric C square on the top left corner of a Fabric O square.

Stitch on the drawn line and trim ¼" away from the seam.

Repeat on the bottom right corner.
Dragonfly Body Unit should measure 3" x 3".

Make one.   Make one.

Assemble Unit.
Top Dragonfly Head Unit should measure 3" x 3".

Make one.

Assemble Unit.
Bottom Dragonfly Head Unit should measure 1 ¾" x 1 ¾".

Make one.

Assemble Unit.
Left Dragonfly Block Unit should measure 4 ¼" x 10 ½".

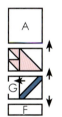 

Make one.

Pretty Playtime Quilts by Elea Lutz · 51

Garden Fairy Sampler Quilt

Assemble Unit.
Middle Dragonfly Block Unit should measure 4 ¼" x 4 ¼".

Make one.

Assemble Unit.
Right Dragonfly Block Unit should measure 6 ¾" x 10 ½".

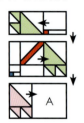 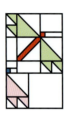

Make one.

Assemble Unit.
Dragonfly Block Unit should measure 10 ½" x 10 ½".

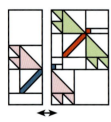 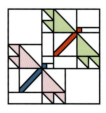

Make one.

Assemble Block.
Dragonfly Block should measure 12 ½" x 12 ½".

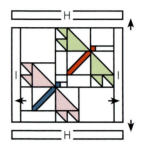 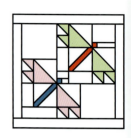

Make one.

Block 2
Bow Block

Cutting Instructions

Background	A	8 - 3 ¾" x 4 ¾" rectangles
	B	4 - 2" x 4" rectangles
	C	1 - 1 ½" x 12 ½" rectangle
	D	2 - 1 ½" x 6" rectangles
	E	4 - 1 ¼" x 2" rectangles
	F	8 - 1 ¼" squares
Bow (Four Fabrics)	G	1 - 3 ¾" x 4 ¾" rectangle (from each Fabric G)
	H	1 - 3 ¾" x 4 ¾" rectangle (from each Fabric H)
	I	2 - 2 ½" squares (from each Fabric I)
	J	1 - 1 ¾" x 2" rectangle (from each Fabric J)

Piecing Instructions:

Draw a diagonal line on the wrong side of the Fabric F squares.

With right sides facing, layer a Fabric F square on the top right corner of a Fabric I square.

Stitch on the drawn line and trim ¼" away from the seam.

Partial Top Bow Unit should measure 2 ½" x 2 ½".

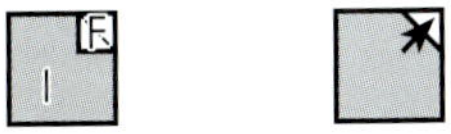

Make two from each Fabric I.
Make eight total.

• •

Assemble Unit.
Top Bow Unit should measure 2 ½" x 6".

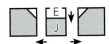

Make one from each Fabric J.
Make four total.

Draw a diagonal line on the right side of the Fabric G rectangles and the wrong side of four Fabric A rectangles.

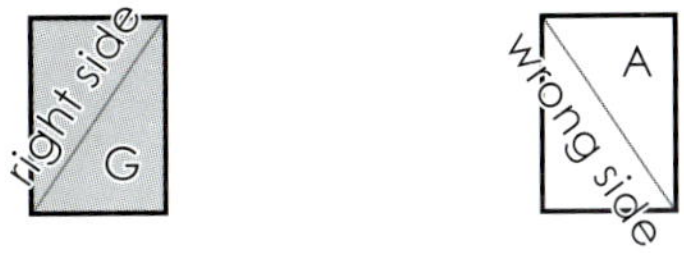

With right sides facing, layer a marked Fabric A rectangle with a marked Fabric G rectangle matching drawn lines.

Stitch on the drawn line and trim ¼" above the seam.

Using the template, trim the Left Streamer Unit to measure 2 ½" x 4".

Follow placement instructions on the template.

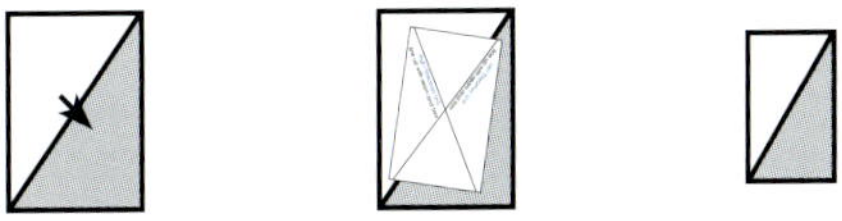

Make one from each Fabric G.
Make four total.

Garden Fairy Sampler Quilt

Draw a diagonal line on the right side of the remaining Fabric A rectangles and the wrong side of the Fabric H rectangles.

With right sides facing, layer a marked Fabric H rectangle with a marked Fabric A rectangle matching drawn lines.

Stitch on the drawn line and trim ¼" below the seam.

Using the template, trim the Right Streamer Unit to measure 2 ½" x 4".

Follow placement instructions on the template.

Make one from each Fabric H.
Make four total.

Assemble Unit.
Bottom Bow Unit should measure 4" x 6".

Make four.

Assemble Unit.
Bow Unit should measure 6" x 6".

Make four.

Assemble Block.
Bow Block should measure 12 ½" x 12 ½".

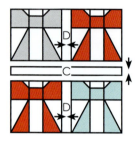 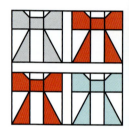

Make one.

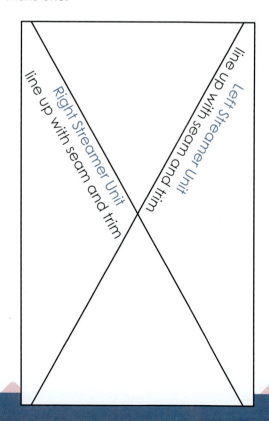

54 · Pretty Playtime Quilts by Elea Lutz

Block 3
Tooth Fairy Block

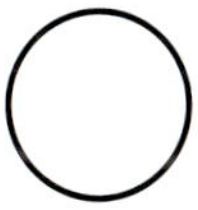

Cheek Template
Fabric T - Cut 2

mouth

braid

Cutting Instructions

Background	A	1 - 3 ½" x 5" rectangle
	B	1 - 3 ½" x 5" rectangle
	C	2 - 3 ½" squares
	D	2 - 2 ½" x 4 ⅞" rectangles
	E	2 - 2" x 7 ½" rectangles
	F	2 - 2" squares
	G	2 - 1 ½" x 3 ½" rectangles
	H	2 - 1 ½" squares
	I	1 - 1 ¼" x 2 ½" rectangle
Skin	J	1 - 3 ½" square
	K	1 - 2 ⅜" square
	L	2 - 2" squares
	M	2 - 1 ¾" squares
Hair and Shoes	N	2 - 2" squares
	O	1 - 1 ½" x 3 ½" rectangle
	P	2 - 1 ¼" x 1 ¾" rectangles
Fairy Wings	Q	1 - 3 ½" x 5" rectangle
	R	1 - 3 ½" x 5" rectangle
	S	1 - 2 ⅜" square
Fairy Cheeks	T	2 - Applique Pieces
Pink Dress	U	1 - 2" x 3 ½" rectangle
Aqua Dress	V	1 - 2" x 3 ½" rectangle
	W	2 - 2" squares
Blue Dress	X	1 - 3 ½" x 12 ½" rectangle
	Y	2 - 3 ½" squares
Buttons		2 - ³⁄₁₆" Black Buttons

Pretty Playtime Quilts by Elea Lutz · 55

Garden Fairy Sampler Quilt

Piecing Instructions:

Mark a dot 3 ½" over from the bottom left corner on the wrong side of the Fabric A rectangle.

Draw a line from the top left corner to the dot.

With right sides facing, layer the Fabric A rectangle with the Fabric Q rectangle.

Stitch on the drawn line and trim ¼" away from the seam.

Left Partial Wing Unit should measure 3 ½" x 6 ½".

Make one.

• •

Draw a diagonal line on the wrong side of the Fabric L squares and the Fabric W squares.

With right sides facing, layer a Fabric L square on the bottom left corner of a Fabric Y square.

Stitch on the drawn line and trim ¼" away from the seam.

Repeat on the bottom right corner with a Fabric W square.

Bottom Left Wing Unit should measure 3 ½" x 3 ½".

Make one.

Draw a diagonal line on the wrong side of the Bottom Left Wing Unit.

Pay close attention to unit placement.

Make one.

• •

Draw a diagonal line on the wrong side of the Fabric F squares.

With right sides facing, layer a Fabric F square on the top right corner of the Left Partial Wing Unit.

Stitch on the drawn line and trim ¼" away from the seam.

Repeat on the bottom end with the Bottom Left Wing Unit.

Left Wing Unit should measure 3 ½" x 6 ½".

Make one.

56 · Pretty Playtime Quilts by Elea Lutz

Mark a dot 3 ½" over from the bottom right corner on the wrong side of the Fabric B rectangle.

Draw a line from the top right corner to the dot.

With right sides facing, layer the marked Fabric B rectangle with the Fabric R rectangle.

Stitch on the drawn line and trim ¼" away from the seam.

Right Partial Wing Unit should measure 3 ½" x 6 ½".

Make one.

• •

With right sides facing, layer a Fabric W square on the bottom left corner of a Fabric Y square.

Stitch on the drawn line and trim ¼" away from the seam.

Repeat on the bottom right corner with a Fabric L square.

Bottom Right Wing Unit should measure 3 ½" x 3 ½".

Make one.

Draw a diagonal line on the wrong side of the Bottom Right Wing Unit.

Pay close attention to unit placement.

Make one.

• •

With right sides facing, layer a Fabric F square on the top left corner of the Right Partial Wing Unit.

Stitch on the drawn line and trim ¼" away from the seam.

Repeat on the bottom end with the Bottom Right Wing Unit.

Right Wing Unit should measure 3 ½" x 6 ½".

Make one.

• •

Draw a diagonal line on the wrong side of the Fabric K square.

With right sides facing, layer the Fabric K square with the Fabric S square.

Stitch ¼" from each side of the drawn line.

Cut apart on the marked line.

Half Square Triangle Unit should measure 2" x 2".

Make two.

Pretty Playtime Quilts by Elea Lutz · 57

Garden Fairy Sampler Quilt

Draw a diagonal line on the wrong side of the Half Square Triangle Units.

Make two.

• •

Draw a diagonal line on the wrong side of the Fabric N squares.

With right sides facing, layer a Fabric N square on the top left corner of the Fabric J square.

Stitch on the drawn line and trim ¼" away from the seam.

Repeat on the top right corner with a Fabric N square and the bottom corners with the Half Square Triangle Units.

Pay close attention to unit placement.

Face Unit should measure 3 ½" x 3 ½".

Make one.

• •

Draw a diagonal line on the wrong side of the Fabric H squares.

With right sides facing, layer a Fabric H square on one end of the Fabric O rectangle.

Stitch on the drawn line and trim ¼" away from the seam.

Repeat on the opposite end.

Partial Hair Unit should measure 1 ½" x 3 ½".

Make one.

Assemble Unit.

Hair Unit should measure 1 ½" x 9 ½".

Make one.

• •

Assemble Unit.

Top Partial Fairy Unit should measure 6 ½" x 9 ½".

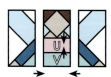

Make one.

• •

Assemble Unit.

Top Fairy Unit should measure 7 ½" x 12 ½".

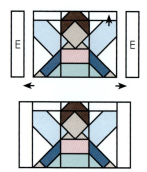

Make one.

Draw a diagonal line on the wrong side of the Fabric C squares.

With right sides facing, layer a Fabric C square on one end of the Fabric X rectangle.

Stitch on the drawn line and trim ¼" away from the seam.

Repeat on opposite end.

Skirt Unit should measure 3 ½" x 12 ½".

Make one.

Assemble Unit.

Bottom Fairy Unit should measure 2 ½" x 12 ½".

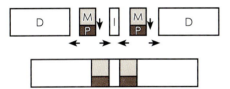

Make one.

Assemble Block.

Tooth Fairy Block should measure 12 ½" x 12 ½".

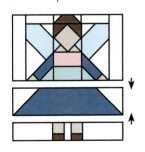 

Make one.

Using the Cheek Template on page 55, trace the cheeks on the fabric. Templates are actual size and do not include a ¼" seam allowance.

Applique two cheeks.

Attach buttons.

To add the mouth and braids, use the templates on page 55.

Use three strands of embroidery floss and a backstitch.

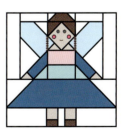

Pretty Playtime Quilts by Elea Lutz · 59

Garden Fairy Sampler Quilt

Block 4
Star Block

Cutting Instructions

Background	A	8 - 2 ⅜" squares
	B	16 - 2" x 3 ½" rectangles
	C	16 - 2" squares
Stars (Two Fabrics)	D	2 - 2 ⅜" squares (from each Fabric D)
	E	8 - 2" squares (from each Fabric E)
Stars (Two Fabrics)	F	2 - 2 ⅜" squares (from each Fabric F)
	G	8 - 2" squares (from each Fabric G)

Piecing Instructions:

Draw a diagonal line on the wrong side of the Fabric E squares.

With right sides facing, layer a Fabric E square on one end of a Fabric B rectangle.

Stitch on the drawn line and trim ¼" away from the seam.

Repeat on the opposite end.
Lime/Pink Flying Geese Unit should measure 2" x 3 ½".

Make four.   Make four.

Draw a diagonal line on the wrong side of the Fabric G squares.

With right sides facing, layer a Fabric G square on one end of a Fabric B rectangle.

Stitch on the drawn line and trim ¼" away from the seam.

Repeat on the opposite end.
Pink/Aqua Flying Geese Unit should measure 2" x 3 ½".

Make four.   Make four.

Draw a diagonal line on the wrong side of the Fabric A squares.

With right sides facing, layer a Fabric A square with a Fabric D square.

Stitch ¼" from each side of the drawn line.

Cut apart on the marked line.

Lime/Pink Half Square Triangle Unit should measure 2" x 2".

Make four.   Make four.

With right sides facing, layer a Fabric A square with a Fabric F square.

Stitch ¼" from each side of the drawn line.

Cut apart on the marked line.

Pink/Aqua Half Square Triangle Unit should measure 2" x 2".

Make four.   Make four.

Assemble Unit.

Center Star Unit should measure 3 ½" x 3 ½".

  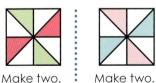

Make two.   Make two.

Assemble Unit.

Lime/Pink Star Unit should measure 6 ½" x 6 ½".

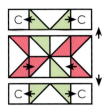

Make two.

Assemble Unit.

Pink/Aqua Star Unit should measure 6 ½" x 6 ½".

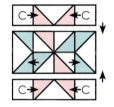

Make two.

Assemble Block.

Star Block should measure 12 ½" x 12 ½".

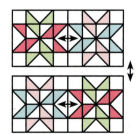 

Make one.

Pretty Playtime Quilts by Elea Lutz · 61

Garden Fairy Sampler Quilt

Block 5
Bowtie Block

Cutting Instructions

Background	A	18 - 2 ½" squares
Bowtie	B	2 - 2 ½" squares (from each Fabric B)
(Nine Fabrics)	C	2 - 1 ½" squares (from each Fabric C)

Piecing Instructions:

Draw a diagonal line on the wrong side of the Fabric C squares.

With right sides facing, layer a Fabric C square on the bottom right corner of a Fabric A square.

Stitch on the drawn line and trim ¼" away from the seam.

Partial Bowtie Unit should measure 2 ½" x 2 ½".

Make two from each Fabric C.
Make eighteen total.

Assemble Unit.
Bowtie Unit should measure 4 ½" x 4 ½".

Make nine.

Assemble Block.
Bowtie Block should measure 12 ½" x 12 ½".

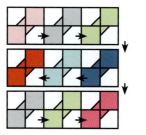 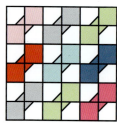

Make one.

Block 6
Cottage Block

Cutting Instructions

Background	A	1 - 5 ½" square
	B	1 - 2 ½" x 4 ½" rectangle
	C	2 - 1 ½" x 11 ½" rectangles
	D	1 - 1 ½" x 5 ½" rectangle
	E	2 - 1" x 12 ½" rectangles
Chimney and Cottage Siding	F	1 - 3 ½" x 4 ½" rectangle
	G	2 - 1 ½" x 2 ½" rectangles
Roof	H	1 - 5 ½" x 10 ½" rectangle
Cottage	I	1 - 2 ½" x 5" rectangle
	J	2 - 1 ¾" x 2 ½" rectangles
	K	1 - 1 ½" x 8 ½" rectangle
	L	1 - 1 ½" x 5" rectangle
	M	1 - 1 ½" x 4 ¾" rectangle
	N	1 - 1 ¼" x 4" rectangle
Window	O	1 - 2 ½" square
Door	P	1 - 3" x 4 ¾" rectangle
Cottage Siding (Four Fabrics)	Q	1 - 1 ½" x 2 ½" rectangle (from each Fabric Q)
Button		1 - ⅝" Pink Button

Piecing Instructions:

Assemble Unit.
Chimney Unit should measure 5 ½" x 5 ½".

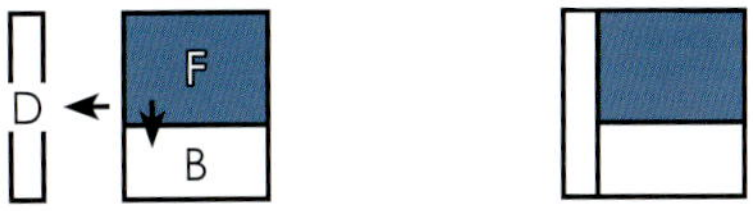

Make one.

Draw a diagonal line on the wrong side of the Chimney Unit.
Pay close attention to unit placement.

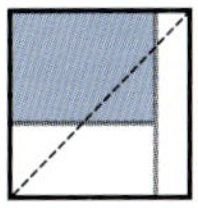

Make one.

Pretty Playtime Quilts by Elea Lutz

Garden Fairy Sampler Quilt

Draw a diagonal line on the wrong side of the Fabric A square.

With right sides facing, layer the Chimney Unit on the left end of the Fabric H rectangle.

Stitch on the drawn line and trim ¼" away from the seam.

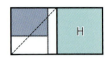 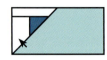

Repeat on the opposite end with the Fabric A square.

Roof Unit should measure 5 ½" x 10 ½".

 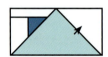

Make one.

• •

Assemble Unit.

Window Unit should measure 5" x 5 ½".

Make one.

• •

Assemble Unit.

Door Unit should measure 4" x 5 ½".

Make one.

Assemble Unit.

Partial Bottom Cottage Unit should measure 6 ½" x 8 ½".

Make one.

• •

Assemble Unit.

Bottom Cottage Unit should measure 6 ½" x 10 ½".

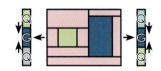 

Make one.

• •

Assemble Unit.

Cottage Unit should measure 10 ½" x 11 ½".

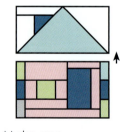 

Make one.

Assemble Block.
Cottage Block should measure 12 ½" x 12 ½".

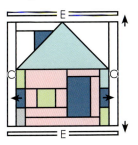 

Make one.

• • • • • • • • • • • • • • • • • •

Attach button.

Pretty Playtime Quilts by Elea Lutz · 65

Garden Fairy Sampler Quilt

**Block 7
Teapot Block**

Cutting Instructions

Background	A	1 - 3 ¼" x 7 ½" rectangle
	B	1 - 3" x 5 ¾" rectangle
	C	1 - 2 ½" x 5 ½" rectangle
	D	1 - 2 ½" square
	E	6 - 2" squares
	F	1 - 1 ¾" x 3 ½" rectangle
	G	1 - 1 ¾" x 3" rectangle
	H	1 - 1 ½" x 12 ½" rectangle
	I	1 - 1 ½" x 2 ½" rectangle
	J	1 - 1 ½" square
	K	1 - 1 ¼" x 3 ½" rectangle
	L	1 - 1 ¼" x 3" rectangle
	M	4 - 1 ¼" squares
Teapot	N	1 - 6 ½" x 8" rectangle (fussy cut)
	O	1 - 2 ½" square
	P	1 - 1 ½" x 3" rectangle
	Q	3 - 1 ½" x 2 ½" rectangles
Teapot Lid	R	1 - 2" x 8" rectangle
	S	1 - 1 ¼" x 2" rectangle
Heart	T	2 - 2" x 2 ¾" rectangles

66 · Pretty Playtime Quilts by Elea Lutz

Piecing Instructions:

Draw a diagonal line on the wrong side of the Fabric M squares and the Fabric E squares.

With right sides facing, layer a Fabric M square on the top left corner of a Fabric T rectangle.

Stitch on the drawn line and trim ¼" away from the seam.

Repeat on the top right corner with a Fabric M square and the bottom end with a Fabric E square.

Partial Heart Unit should measure 2" x 2 ¾".

Make one. Make one.

Assemble Unit.

Heart Unit should measure 2 ¾" x 3 ½".

Make one.

Assemble Unit.

Top Lid Unit should measure 1 ¼" x 7 ½".

Make one.

Assemble Unit.

Top Teapot Unit should measure 4" x 10 ½".

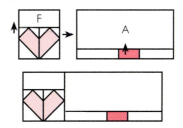

Make one.

Draw a diagonal line on the wrong side of the Fabric J square.

With right sides facing, layer the Fabric J square on the right end of the Fabric P rectangle.

Stitch on the drawn line and trim ¼" away from the seam.

Top Spout Unit should measure 1 ½" x 3".

Make one.

Draw a diagonal line on the wrong side of the Fabric O square.

With right sides facing, layer the Fabric O square on the top right corner of the Fabric B rectangle.

Stitch on the drawn line and trim ¼" away from the seam.

Bottom Spout Unit should measure 3" x 5 ¾".

Make one.

Garden Fairy Sampler Quilt

With right sides facing, layer a Fabric E square on one end of the Fabric R rectangle.

Stitch on the drawn line and trim ¼" away from the seam.

Repeat on the opposite end.

Bottom Lid Unit should measure 2" x 8".

Make one.

• •

With right sides facing, layer a Fabric E square on the bottom left corner of the Fabric N rectangle.

Stitch on the drawn line and trim ¼" away from the seam.

Repeat on the bottom right corner.

Bottom Teapot Unit should measure 6 ½" x 8".

Make one.

• •

Assemble Unit.

Spout Unit should measure 8" x 10 ½".

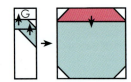 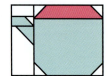

Make one.

Assemble Unit.

Handle Unit should measure 2 ½" x 11 ½".

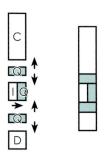

Make one.

• •

Assemble Unit.

Teapot Unit should measure 11 ½" x 12 ½".

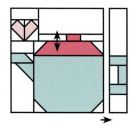 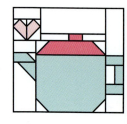

Make one.

• •

Assemble Block.

Teapot Block should measure 12 ½" x 12 ½".

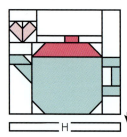 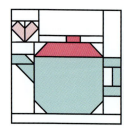

Make one.

Block 8
Strawberry Block

Cutting Instructions

Background	A	1 - 2" x 12 ½" rectangle
	B	8 - 2 ¼" squares
	C	8 - 1 ¼" x 2 ¾" rectangles
	D	2 - 1" x 5 ¾" rectangles
Strawberries (Two Fabrics)	E	2 - 3 ¾" x 5 ¾" rectangles (from each Fabric E)
	F	2 - 3" squares (from each Fabric F)
	G	3 - 2 ⅝" squares (from each Fabric G)
Strawberry Stems	H	3 - 3" squares
	I	4 - 1 ¼" squares

Piecing Instructions:

Assemble Unit.
Stem Unit should measure 1 ¼" x 5 ¾".

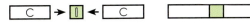

Make four.

• •

Cut the Fabric G squares on the diagonal once.

Make six. Make six.

Cut the Fabric H squares and the Fabric F squares on the diagonal twice.
You will not use all Fabric F triangles.

Make twelve. Make eight. Make eight.

• •

Assemble Unit.

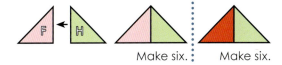

Make six. Make six.

Pretty Playtime Quilts by Elea Lutz

Garden Fairy Sampler Quilt

Assemble Unit.
Partial Strawberry Top Unit should measure 2 ¼" x 2 ¼".

Make six.   Make six.

Draw a diagonal line on the wrong side of the Fabric B squares.

With right sides facing, layer a Fabric B square on the bottom left corner of a Fabric E rectangle.

Stitch on the drawn line and trim ¼" away from the seam.

Repeat on the bottom right corner.
Bottom Strawberry Unit should measure 3 ¾" x 5 ¾".

Make two.   Make two.

Assemble Unit.
Strawberry Unit should measure 5 ¾" x 6 ¼".

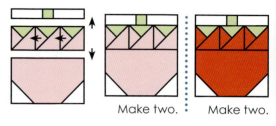

Make two.   Make two.

Assemble Unit.
Partial Strawberry Block Unit should measure 5 ¾" x 12 ½".

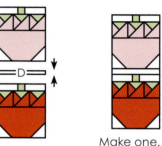

Make one.   Make one.

Assemble Block.
Strawberry Block should measure 12 ½" x 12 ½".

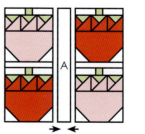 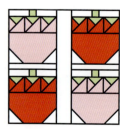

Make one.

Block 9
Kitty Cat Block

Cutting Instructions

Background	A	2 - 2 ½" x 3" rectangles
	B	2 - 2" x 12" rectangles
	C	8 - 1 ¾" squares
	D	1 - 1 ½" x 2 ½" rectangle
	E	6 - 1 ½" squares
	F	2 - 1 ½" squares
	G	1 - 1" x 12 ½" rectangle
Cat Face and Ears	H	1 - 7 ½" x 10 ½" rectangle
	I	2 - 1 ½" x 3" rectangles
Hat	J	1 - 2 ½" x 9 ½" rectangle
Bowtie	K	2 - 3" squares
Cat Eyes	L	2 - Applique Pieces
Cat Cheeks	M	2 - Applique Pieces
Cat Nose	N	1 - Applique Piece
⅝" White Ric Rac		1 - 10 ½" strip

Piecing Instructions:

Draw a diagonal line on the wrong side of the Fabric E squares.

With right sides facing, layer a Fabric E square on one end of a Fabric I rectangle.

Stitch on the drawn line and trim ¼" away from the seam.

Repeat on the opposite end.
Cat Ear Unit should measure 1 ½" x 3".

Make two.

Assemble Unit.
Cat Ears Unit should measure 1 ½" x 9 ½".

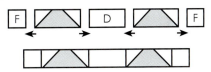

Make one.

Garden Fairy Sampler Quilt

Using the Eye Template, Nose Template and Cheek Template, trace the facial features on the fabric. Templates are actual size and do not include a ¼" seam allowance.

Applique two eyes, one nose and two cheeks on the Fabric H rectangle.

Trim Partial Cat Face Unit to measure 6 ½" x 9 ½".

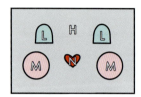

Make one.

• •

With right sides facing, layer a Fabric E square on the bottom left corner of the Partial Cat Face Unit.

Stitch on the drawn line and trim ¼" away from the seam.

Repeat on the bottom right corner.

Cat Face Unit should measure 6 ½" x 9 ½".

Make one.

Draw a diagonal line on the wrong side of the Fabric C squares.

With right sides facing, layer a Fabric C square on one corner of a Fabric K square.

Stitch on the drawn line and trim ¼" away from the seam.

Repeat on the remaining corners.

Partial Bowtie Unit should measure 3" x 3".

Make two.

Nose Template
Fabric N
Cut 1

Eye Template
Fabric L
Cut 2

Cheek Template
Fabric M
Cut 2

Assemble Unit.
Bowtie Unit should measure 3" x 9 ½".

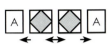

Make one.

- -

Assemble Unit.
Partial Cat Unit should measure 9 ½" x 12".

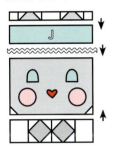 

Make one.

- -

Assemble Unit.
Kitty Cat Unit should measure 12 ½" x 12 ½".

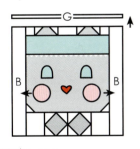 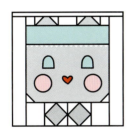

Make one.

To add the eyelashes and mouth, use the templates below.

Use three strands of embroidery floss and a backstitch.

Kitty Cat Block should measure 12 ½" x 12 ½".

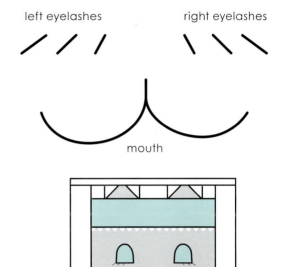

Make one.

Pretty Playtime Quilts by Elea Lutz · 73

Garden Fairy Sampler Quilt

Block 10
Pinwheel Block

Cutting Instructions

Background	A	18 - 2 ⅞" squares
Outer Pinwheels (Two Fabrics)	B	8 - 2 ⅞" squares (from each Fabric B)
Inner Pinwheel	C	2 - 2 ⅞" squares

Piecing Instructions:

Draw a diagonal line on the wrong side of the Fabric A squares.

With right sides facing, layer a Fabric A square with a Fabric B square.

Stitch ¼" from each side of the drawn line.

Cut apart on the marked line.

Pink/Aqua Half Square Triangle Unit should measure 2 ½" x 2 ½".

Make sixteen.   Make sixteen.

With right sides facing, layer a Fabric A square with a Fabric C square.

Stitch ¼" from each side of the drawn line.

Cut apart on the marked line.

Blue Half Square Triangle Unit should measure 2 ½" x 2 ½".

Make four.

Assemble Unit.
Outer Pinwheel Unit should measure 4 ½" x 4 ½".

Make four.   Make four.

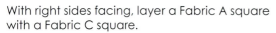

Assemble Unit.
Inner Pinwheel Unit should measure 4 ½" x 4 ½".

Make one.

Assemble Block.
Pinwheel Block should measure 12 ½" x 12 ½".

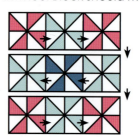 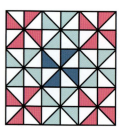

Make one.

Block 11
Basket Block

Cutting Instructions

Background	A	1 - 4 ¾" square
	B	1 - 4" square
	C	1 - 3 ⅜" square
	D	2 - 2 ¼" x 6 ¼" rectangles
	E	2 - 1 ¾" x 5" rectangles
	F	2 - 1 ¾" x 4 ¾" rectangles
	G	2 - 1 ½" x 5 ½" rectangles
Blue Basket Bottom and Handle	H	1 - 3 ⅜" square
	I	2 - 3" x 5 ½" rectangles
	J	2 - 1 ¾" x 5" rectangles
	K	2 - 1 ¾" x 3" rectangles
Aqua Basket Bottom	L	2 - 3 ⅜" squares
	M	4 - 3" squares
Bow	N	1 - 4 ¾" square
Berries	O	3 - Applique Pieces (fussy cut)
	P	1 - Applique Piece (fussy cut)

Piecing Instructions:

Cut the Fabric A square and the Fabric N square on the diagonal twice.

You will not use all the Fabric A triangles and Fabric N triangles.

Make four.   Make four.

• • • • • • • • • • • • • • • • • •

Assemble Unit.

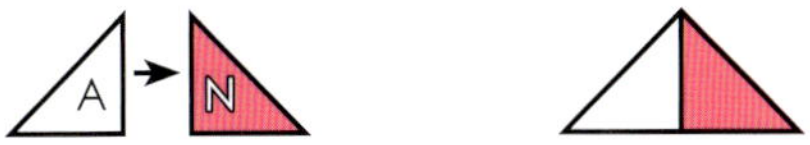

Make two.

Assemble Unit.
Bow Unit should measure 4" x 4".

Make one.

• •

Assemble Unit.
Partial Left Handle Unit should measure 3" x 6 ¼".

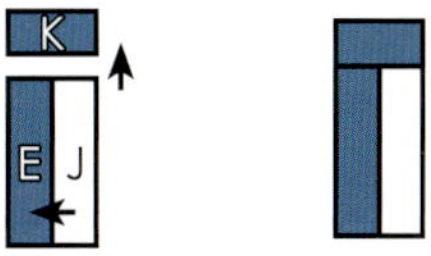

Make one.

Garden Fairy Sampler Quilt

Assemble Unit.
Left Handle Unit should measure 4 ¾" x 7 ½".

Make one.

Assemble Unit.
Partial Right Handle Unit should measure 3" x 6 ¼".

Make one.

Assemble Unit.
Right Handle Unit should measure 4 ¾" x 7 ½".

Make one.

Assemble Unit.
Hourglass Unit should measure 7 ½" x 12 ½".

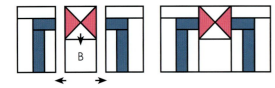

Make one.

Draw a diagonal line on the wrong side of the Fabric C square.
With right sides facing, layer the Fabric C square with a Fabric L square.
Stitch ¼" from each side of the drawn line.
Cut apart on the marked line.
White Half Square Triangle Unit should measure 3" x 3".

Make two.

Draw a diagonal line on the wrong side of the remaining Fabric L square.
With right sides facing, layer the Fabric L square with the Fabric H square.
Stitch ¼" from each side of the drawn line.
Cut apart on the marked line.
Blue Half Square Triangle Unit should measure 3" x 3".

Make two.

Draw a diagonal line on the wrong side of the Fabric M squares.
With right sides facing, layer a Fabric M square on one end of a Fabric I rectangle.
Stitch on the drawn line and trim ¼" away from the seam.

Repeat on the opposite end.
Flying Geese Unit should measure 3" x 5 ½".

Make two.

76 · Pretty Playtime Quilts by Elea Lutz

Assemble Unit.
Bottom Basket Unit should measure
5 ½" x 10 ½".

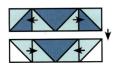 

Make one.

• •

Assemble Unit.
Basket Unit should measure 12 ½" x 12 ½".

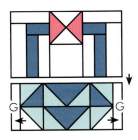 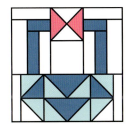

Make one.

• •

Using the Large Berry Template and Small Berry Template, trace the berries on the fabric. Templates are actual size and do not include a ¼" seam allowance.

Applique three large berries and one small berry on the Basket Unit.

Basket Block should measure 12 ½" x 12 ½".

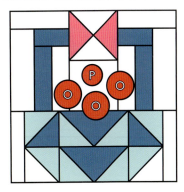
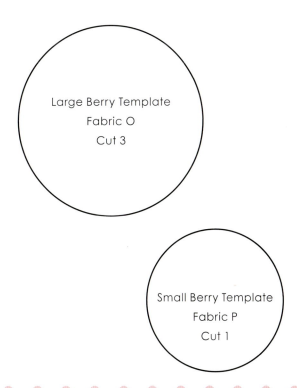

Make one.

Pretty Playtime Quilts by Elea Lutz

Garden Fairy Sampler Quilt

Block 12
Butterfly Block

Cutting Instructions

Background	A	4 - 3 ⅝" squares
	B	24 - 1 ⅞" squares
	C	1 - 1 ½" x 12 ½" rectangle
	D	2 - 1 ½" x 6" rectangles
Top Wings (Two Fabrics)	E	2 - 3 ⅝" squares (from each Fabric E)
Bottom Wings (Two Fabrics)	F	4 - 3 ¼" squares (from each Fabric F)

Piecing Instructions:

Draw a diagonal line on the wrong side of the Fabric A squares.

With right sides facing, layer a Fabric A square with a Fabric E square.

Stitch ¼" from each side of the drawn line.

Cut apart on the marked line.

Half Square Triangle Unit should measure 3 ¼" x 3 ¼".

Make four.   Make four.

Draw a diagonal line on the wrong side of the Fabric B squares.

With right sides facing, layer a Fabric B square on the top left corner of a Fabric F square.

Stitch on the drawn line and trim ¼" away from the seam.

Repeat on the bottom left and bottom right corners.

Bottom Wing Unit should measure 3 ¼" x 3 ¼".

Make four.   Make four.

78 · Pretty Playtime Quilts by Elea Lutz

Assemble Unit.
Butterfly Unit should measure 6" x 6".

Make two.　　Make two.

Assemble Block.
Butterfly Block should measure 12 ½" x 12 ½".

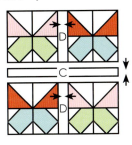 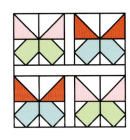

Make one.

Pretty Playtime Quilts by Elea Lutz · 79

Garden Fairy Sampler Quilt

Flower Rows

Cutting Instructions

Background	A	84 - 2 ½" squares
	B	84 - 2 ¼" x 2 ½" rectangles
	C	126 - 1 ½" squares
	D	42 - 1 ¼" x 2" rectangles
	E	84 - 1" x 4" rectangles
	F	21 - 1" x 3 ½" rectangles
Tulip Flower and Posy Stem (Three Fabrics)	G	7 - 3 ¼" x 3 ½" rectangles (from each Fabric G)
	H	7 - 2 ½" x 4 ½" rectangles (from each Fabric H)
	I	14 - 2 ½" squares (from each Fabric I)
	J	28 - 1 ¼" squares (from each Fabric J)
	K	7 - 1" x 2 ½" rectangles (from each Fabric K)
Posy Flower and Tulip Stem (Three Fabrics)	L	7 - 3 ½" squares (from each Fabric L)
	M	7 - 2 ½" x 4 ½" rectangles (from each Fabric M)
	N	14 - 2 ½" squares (from each Fabric N)
	O	7 - 1" x 2 ½" rectangles (from each Fabric O)

Tulip Blocks:

Draw a diagonal line on the wrong side of the Fabric J squares.

With right sides facing, layer a Fabric J square on one end of a Fabric D rectangle.

Stitch on the drawn line and trim ¼" away from the seam.

Repeat on the opposite end.
Tulip Flying Geese Unit should measure 1 ¼" x 2".

Make fourteen from each Fabric J.
Make forty-two total.

Assemble Unit.
Top Tulip Unit should measure 1 ¼" x 3 ½".

Make twenty-one.

Draw a diagonal line on the wrong side of the Fabric C squares.

With right sides facing, layer a Fabric C square on the bottom left corner of a Fabric G rectangle.

Stitch on the drawn line and trim ¼" away from the seam.

Repeat on the bottom right corner.
Bottom Tulip Unit should measure 3 ¼" x 3 ½".

Make seven from each Fabric G.
Make twenty-one total.

Assemble Unit.
Tulip Unit should measure 4" x 4 ½".

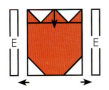

Make twenty-one.

Assemble Unit.
Partial Top Tulip Stem Unit should measure 2 ½" x 4 ½".

Make seven from each Fabric O.
Make twenty-one total.

Draw a diagonal line on the wrong side of the Fabric N squares.

With right sides facing, layer a matching Fabric N square on one end of a Partial Top Tulip Stem Unit.

Stitch on the drawn line and trim ¼" away from the seam.

Repeat on the opposite end.
Top Tulip Stem Unit should measure 2 ½" x 4 ½".

Make seven from each Fabric O.
Make twenty-one total.

Draw a diagonal line on the wrong side of the Fabric A squares.

With right sides facing, layer a Fabric A square on one end of a Fabric M rectangle.

Stitch on the drawn line and trim ¼" away from the seam.

Repeat on the opposite end.
Bottom Tulip Stem Unit should measure 2 ½" x 4 ½".

Make seven from each Fabric M.
Make twenty-one total.

Pretty Playtime Quilts by Elea Lutz

Garden Fairy Sampler Quilt

Assemble Block.
Tulip Block should measure 4 ½" x 8".

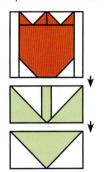 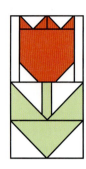

Make twenty-one.

Posy Blocks:

With right sides facing, layer a Fabric C square on the top left corner of a Fabric L square.

Stitch on the drawn line and trim ¼" away from the seam.

Repeat on the remaining corners.
Partial Posy Unit should measure 3 ½" x 3 ½".

Make seven from each Fabric L.
Make twenty-one total.

Assemble Unit.
Posy Unit should measure 4" x 4 ½".

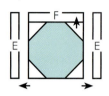

Make seven from each Fabric L.
Make twenty-one total.

Assemble Unit.
Partial Top Posy Stem Unit should measure 2 ½" x 4 ½".

Make seven from each Fabric K.
Make twenty-one total.

Draw a diagonal line on the wrong side of the Fabric I squares.

With right sides facing, layer a matching Fabric I square on one end of a Partial Top Posy Stem Unit.

Stitch on the drawn line and trim ¼" away from the seam.

Repeat on the opposite end.
Top Posy Stem Unit should measure 2 ½" x 4 ½".

Make seven from each Fabric K.
Make twenty-one total.

With right sides facing, layer a Fabric A square on one end of a Fabric H rectangle.

Stitch on the drawn line and trim ¼" away from the seam.

Repeat on the opposite end.
Bottom Posy Stem Unit should measure 2 ½" x 4 ½".

Make seven from each Fabric H.
Make twenty-one total.

Assemble Block.
Posy Block should measure 4 ½" x 8".

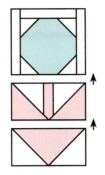 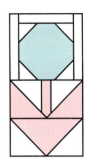

Make twenty-one.

Flower Rows:

Assemble Row.
Flower Row should measure 8" x 56 ½".

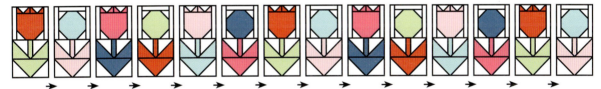

Make one.

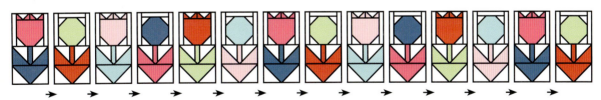

Make one.

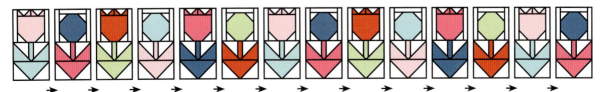

Make one.

Garden Fairy Sampler Quilt

Duck Row

Cutting Instructions

Background	A	1 - 4 ½" square
	B	1 - 3 ½" x 4 ¼" rectangle
	C	5 - 3 ½" squares
	D	1 - 3" x 4 ½" rectangle
	E	5 - 3" x 3 ½" rectangles
	F	1 - 3" square
	G	5 - 2 ½" x 3 ½" rectangles
	H	5 - 2 ½" squares
	I	1 - 2 ¼" x 37" rectangle
	J	1 - 2 ¼" x 10 ¾" rectangle
	K	2 - 2" x 6 ½" rectangles
	L	5 - 1 ¾" x 6 ½" rectangles
	M	1 - 1 ¾" x 3" rectangle
	N	3 - 1 ¾" squares
	O	5 - 1 ½" x 2 ½" rectangles
	P	15 - 1 ½" squares
Lime Baby Ducks and Mama Duck	Q	1 - 4 ¼" square
	R	2 - 3 ½" squares
	S	1 - 2 ½" x 7 ¼" rectangle
	T	2 - 2 ½" squares
	U	2 - 2" x 6" rectangles
	V	4 - 2" squares
	W	2 - 1 ½" squares
	X	4 - 1 ¼" squares

Cutting Instructions

Aqua Baby Ducks	Y	3 - 3 ½" squares
	Z	3 - 2" x 6" rectangles
	AA	6 - 2" squares
	BB	6 - 1 ¼" squares
Wings and Beaks	CC	1 - 2 ½" x 3 ¼" rectangle
	DD	5 - 2" x 3" rectangles
	EE	2 - 1 ¾" squares
	FF	10 - 1 ½" squares
Buttons		1 - 7/16" Navy Button
		5 - 3/8" Navy Buttons

84 · Pretty Playtime Quilts by Elea Lutz

Lime Baby Duck Blocks:

Draw a diagonal line on the wrong side of the Fabric P squares.

With right sides facing, layer a Fabric P square on the top left corner of a Fabric R square.

Stitch on the drawn line and trim ¼" away from the seam.

Repeat on the top right corner and bottom left corner.

Lime Baby Duck Head Unit should measure 3 ½" x 3 ½".

Make two.

• •

Draw a diagonal line on the wrong side of the Fabric FF squares.

With right sides facing, layer a Fabric FF square on the top left corner of a Fabric H square.

Stitch on the drawn line and trim ¼" away from the seam.

Repeat on the bottom left corner.

Lime Baby Duck Beak Unit should measure 2 ½" x 2 ½".

Make two.

Assemble Unit.

Top Lime Baby Duck Unit should measure 3 ½" x 8".

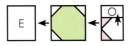

Make two.

• •

Draw a diagonal line on the wrong side of the Fabric X squares.

With right sides facing, layer a Fabric X square on the top left corner of a Fabric DD rectangle.

Stitch on the drawn line and trim ¼" away from the seam.

Repeat on the bottom left corner.

Lime Baby Duck Wing Unit should measure 2" x 3".

Make two.

• •

Assemble Unit.

Partial Lime Baby Duck Body Unit should measure 3 ½" x 6".

Make two.

Pretty Playtime Quilts by Elea Lutz · 85

Garden Fairy Sampler Quilt

Draw a diagonal line on the wrong side of the Fabric C squares.

With right sides facing, layer a Fabric C square on the left end of a Partial Lime Baby Duck Body Unit.

Stitch on the drawn line and trim ¼" away from the seam.

Lime Baby Duck Body Unit should measure 3 ½" x 6".

Make two.

Assemble Block.
Lime Baby Duck Block should measure 6 ½" x 8".

Make two.

Aqua Baby Duck Blocks:

With right sides facing, layer a Fabric P square on the top left corner of a Fabric Y square.

Stitch on the drawn line and trim ¼" away from the seam.

Repeat on the top right corner and bottom left corner.

Aqua Baby Duck Head Unit should measure 3 ½" x 3 ½".

Make three.

With right sides facing, layer a Fabric FF square on the top left corner of a Fabric H square.

Stitch on the drawn line and trim ¼" away from the seam.

Repeat on the bottom left corner.

Aqua Baby Duck Beak Unit should measure 2 ½" x 2 ½".

Make three.

Assemble Unit.
Pay close attention to unit placement.
Top Aqua Baby Duck Unit should measure 3 ½" x 8".

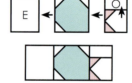 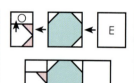

Make two
Left Top Aqua Baby Duck Units.

Make one
Right Top Aqua Baby Duck Unit.

Draw a diagonal line on the wrong side of the Fabric BB squares.

With right sides facing, layer a Fabric BB square on the top left corner of a Fabric DD rectangle.

Stitch on the drawn line and trim ¼" away from the seam.

Repeat on the bottom left corner.

Aqua Baby Duck Wing Unit should measure 2" x 3".

Make three.

· ·

Assemble Unit.

Partial Aqua Baby Duck Body Unit should measure 3 ½" x 6".

Make two
Left Partial Aqua
Baby Duck Body
Units.

Make one
Right Partial
Aqua Baby
Duck Body Unit.

With right sides facing, layer a Fabric C square on the left end of a Left Partial Aqua Baby Duck Body Unit.

Stitch on the drawn line and trim ¼" away from the seam.

Left Aqua Baby Duck Body Unit should measure 3 ½" x 6".

Make two.

· ·

With right sides facing, layer a Fabric C square on the right end of the Right Partial Aqua Baby Duck Body Unit.

Stitch on the drawn line and trim ¼" away from the seam.

Right Aqua Baby Duck Body Unit should measure 3 ½" x 6".

Make one.

· ·

Assemble Block.

Aqua Baby Duck Block should measure 6 ½" x 8".

Make two
Left Aqua
Baby Duck
Blocks.

Make one
Right Aqua
Baby Duck
Block.

Pretty Playtime Quilts by Elea Lutz · 87

Garden Fairy Sampler Quilt

Mama Duck Block:

Draw a diagonal line on the wrong side of the Fabric N squares.

With right sides facing, layer a Fabric N square on the top left corner of the Fabric Q square.

Stitch on the drawn line and trim ¼" away from the seam.

Repeat on the top right corner and bottom left corner.

Mama Duck Head Unit should measure 4 ¼" x 4 ¼".

Make one.

• •

Draw a diagonal line on the wrong side of the Fabric EE squares.

With right sides facing, layer a Fabric EE square on the top left corner of the Fabric F square.

Stitch on the drawn line and trim ¼" away from the seam.

Repeat on the bottom left corner.

Mama Duck Beak Unit should measure 3" x 3".

Make one.

Assemble Unit.

Top Mama Duck Unit should measure 4 ¼" x 9 ¾".

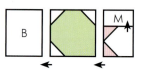 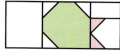

Make one.

• •

Draw a diagonal line on the wrong side of the Fabric W squares.

With right sides facing, layer a Fabric W square on the top left corner of the Fabric CC rectangle.

Stitch on the drawn line and trim ¼" away from the seam.

Repeat on the bottom left corner.

Mama Duck Wing Unit should measure 2 ½" x 3 ¼".

Make one.

• •

Assemble Unit.

Partial Mama Duck Body Unit should measure 4 ½" x 7 ¼".

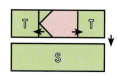 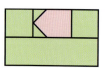

Make one.

Draw a diagonal line on the wrong side of the Fabric A square.

With right sides facing, layer the Fabric A square on the left end of the Partial Mama Duck Body Unit.

Stitch on the drawn line and trim ¼" away from the seam.

Mama Duck Body Unit should measure 4 ½" x 7 ¼".

Make one.

Assemble Block.
Mama Duck Block should measure 8 ¼" x 9 ¾".

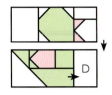 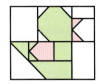

Make one.

Buttons:
Attach buttons.

Make two. Make two.

Make one. Make one.

Duck Row:
Assemble Row.
Duck Row should measure 8 ¼" x 56 ½".

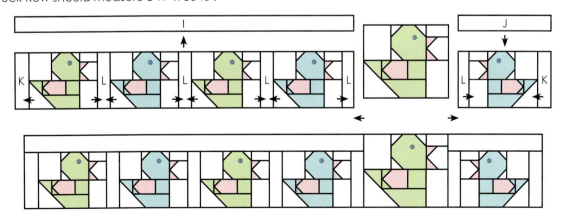

Make one.

Pretty Playtime Quilts by Elea Lutz

Garden Fairy Sampler Quilt

Sampler Finishing

Cutting Instructions

Background	A	112 - 4 ⅛" squares
	B	13 - 2 ½" x WOF strips
	C	9 - 2 ½" x 12 ½" rectangles
	D	9 - 2 ¼" x WOF strips
	E	60 - 2 ¼" squares
	F	4 - 2 ⅛" x WOF strips
	G	6 - 1 ½" x 12 ½" rectangles
	H	8 - 1 ¼" x 4" rectangles
	I	8 - 1 ¼" x 5 ½" rectangles
Border Blocks (Three Pink, Three Blue, Three Aqua and Three Lime Fabrics)	J	15 - 2 ¼" squares (from each Fabric J)
Binding	K	10 - 2 ½" x WOF strips

Quilt Center:

Piece the Fabric D strips end to end.
Subcut into:
    6 - 2 ¼" x 56 ½" strips (Sashing)

Assemble Quilt Center. Press toward the background.
Quilt Center should measure 56 ½" x 77 ¼".

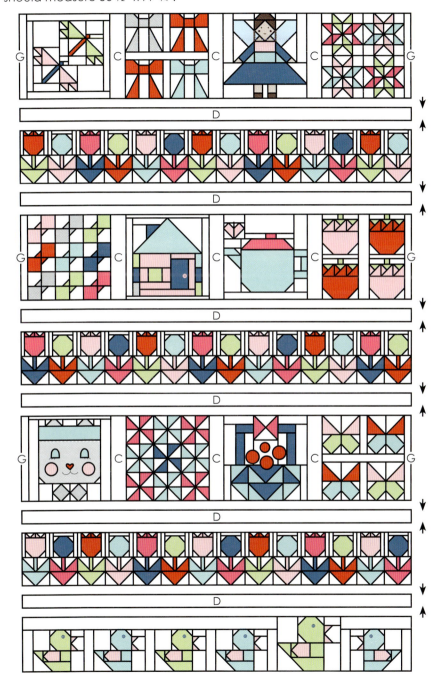

Garden Fairy Sampler Quilt

Borders:
Cut the Fabric A squares on the diagonal once.

Make two hundred twenty-four.

Assemble Unit.
Four Patch Unit should measure 4" x 4".

Make fifteen.   Make fifteen.

Make fifteen.   Make fifteen.

Assemble Block.
Trim Diamond Block to measure 5 ½" x 5 ½".

Make fourteen.   Make fourteen.

 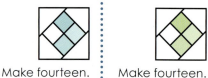

Make fourteen.   Make fourteen.

Assemble Block.
Four Patch Block should measure 5 ½" x 5 ½".

Make one.   Make one.

Make one.   Make one.

92 · Pretty Playtime Quilts by Elea Lutz

Assemble Border.
Second Side Border should measure 5 ½" x 80 ½".

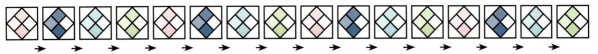

Make one.

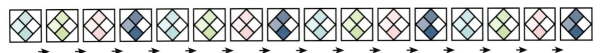

Make one.

Assemble Border.
Second Top and Bottom Border should measure 5 ½" x 70 ½".

Make one.

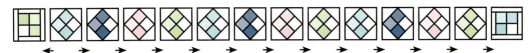

Make one.

Piece the Fabric B strips end to end.
Subcut into:
    2 - 2 ½" x 77 ¼" strips (First Side Borders - B1)
    2 - 2 ½" x 90 ½" strips (Third Side Borders - B2)
    2 - 2 ½" x 74 ½" strips (Third Top and Bottom Borders - B3)

Piece the Fabric F strips end to end.
Subcut into:
    2 - 2 ⅛" x 60 ½" strips (First Top and Bottom Borders)

Garden Fairy Sampler Quilt

Attach First Side Borders and First Top and Bottom Borders.
Attach Second Side Borders and Second Top and Bottom Borders.
Attach Third Side Borders and Third Top and Bottom Borders.
Press toward the background.

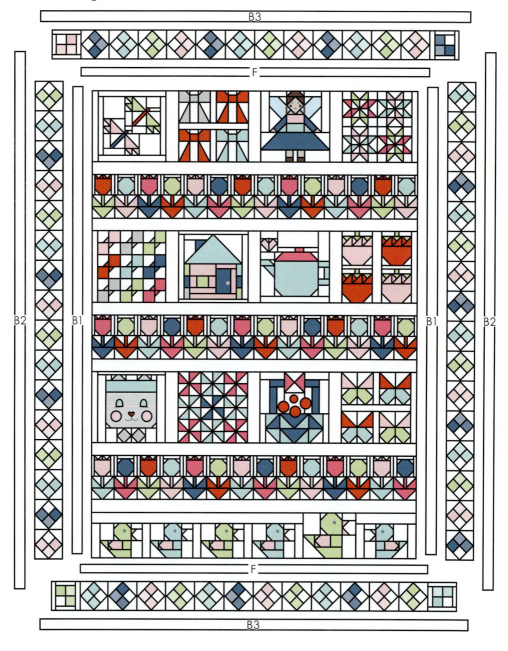

94 · Pretty Playtime Quilts by Elea Lutz

Finishing:

Piece the Fabric K strips end to end for binding.
Quilt and bind as desired.

Furry Friends Quilt

Background	WHITE SOLID
Animal Faces and Ears	SILVER SOLID
Animal Hats	
C5102-BLUE	C5102-GREEN C5102-PINK
Animal Bowties	
C5100-HOTPINK	C5103-GREEN C5105-GRAY
Animal Eyes	
C5100-GRAY	C5104-HOTPINK C5105-AQUA
Animal Noses	C5106-RED
Animal Cheeks	C5103-PINK
Flowers	C5104-PINK
Stems	C5105-GREEN
Binding	C5102-GREEN
Backing	C5100-GRAY

C5100-BLUE

C5100-GRAY

C5100-HOTPINK

C5101-BLUE

C5101-GREEN

C5101-PINK

C5102-BLUE

C5102-GREEN

C5102-PINK

C5103-GREEN

C5103-PINK

C5103-RED

C5104-BLUE

C5104-HOTPINK

C5104-PINK

Tooth Fairy Pillow

Background	WHITE SOLID
Skin	CREAM SOLID
Hair and Shoes	BROWN SOLID
Fairy Wings	AQUA SOLID
Fairy Cheeks	PINK SOLID
Tooth Pocket	C5103-RED
Pink Dress	C5103-PINK
Aqua Dress	C5105-AQUA
Dress Sleeves, Border and Binding	C5106-BLUE
Backing	C5106-BLUE

C5105-AQUA

C5105-GRAY

C5105-GREEN

C5106-AQUA

C5106-BLUE

C5106-RED

96 · Pretty Playtime Quilts by Elea Lutz